Be we  Y0-EKQ-134

Waves

Ebbs and Flows

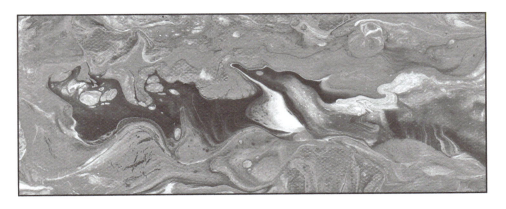

Waves

Waves of ocean
waves of air
waves of invention
waves of hand, in hair
waves of sound
waves of light
waves of energy
waves of despair or delight
waves of people on the move
waves of generations
waves of dance, music, art
waves of ideas and sensations
waves ebb and flow
waves of now and long ago

Linda Varsell Smith

Focus your intention on your dreams,
you wave magic when you set
your heart and mind to it.

Miranda Karr

Waver of Art
Maureen Frank
Formater and Illustrator
@mandalalady.com

Waves of Information
copyright: © 2020
ISBN: 978-1-71691-099-9

Rainbow Communications
471 NW Hemlock Ave.
Corvallis, OR 97330

varsell4@comcast.net

Waver of Poetry
Linda Varsell Smith

Word-waver since childhood with her first poem at six
in rhymed quatrains. She has written ever since
publishing poetry books and chapbooks.
teaching creative writing classes and workshops,
judging and sponsoring poetry contests,
editing Calyx Books for 32 years,
serving on boards for Oregon Poetry Association
and PEN Women of Portland,
part of the Writing the Wrongs to Rights Huddle,
member of poetry critique groups,
avid competitive and cooperative Scrabble player,
appreciates plays, poetry readings, science and arts.
She lives with husband Court in Corvallis, Oregon
in a mini-museum of miniatures

Waves Contents

Waves in the Backyard

Waves of Nature

Quotidian Waves

Waves of Thought

Waves of the Future

Waves of Celebration

Waves of 53

Waves in the Backyard

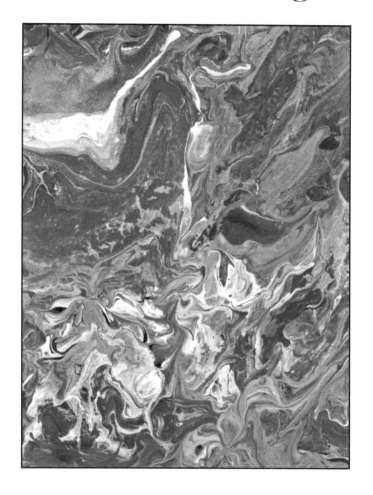

Neither can the wave
that has passed by be recalled,
not the hour which has passed
return again.

Ovid

Backyard Beckoning

Through the window I gaze upon
the backyard. Sock-feet on slate
floor, debating whether to put on shoes.

A butterfly flits by fluttering and muttering
"Come on outside. Join us."
The ripening pears radiate golden.

The wind chimes whisper–" Listen. Closer."
The six sunflowers, facing the sun insist
I want the warmth of the rejuvenating sun.

The pinwheel waffles with the wind—
switches directions, pauses, whirls—
indecisive as I am.

Instead of picking up the blue pillow
for my outside chair, I sit on it
on an inside chair instead.

The windfall apples and hazelnut
husks hug earth, but I am not
seeking grounding somehow.

My spirit wants me to spin my chakras,
breathe in chi, but my body does not
want to make the effort to put on shoes.

It is so yummy-summery, sunny out there.
In here it is shadowy, cool. I want more
layers to warm and energize me.

Why do I turn my back on comfort, healing,
solace and remain inside unfulfilled?
Why do I let my spiraling mind dirge me?

Adrift

After the weekend, the sunflowers
blossomed to five. The unwatered
grass still had a trim-mowing.

The windfall apples bubble on the lawn.
Two boxes left yesterday for a friend's horse.
Two boxes left today for gleaners' pigs.

Bees sniff the reddening, baking apples.
The dandelions are gone except
for one withering straggler near the patio.

I haul the chair from roof-line shade between
canopy shadows to catch the sun-rays
on my back. Hoodie protects my face.

I am despondent over family issues
and gloomy global news. I need warmth.
I need this sunny day to reflect, refocus.

The garbage truck screeches can to can
to pick up and carry away our detritus.
If only it could carry away the garbage I carry.

I'd gladly toss stress, worry, pain, hurt
into a container to haul away. I'm recovering
from a weekend virus and long-on-hold calls.

It is a complex insurance issue which after
hours of calls seem settled for a little while.
I should feel a little lifted. But I don't.

The sun soaks in. Butterflies whisk by.
But the angle I am sitting does not provide
a view of birds or the sunflowers.

After a half hour, I decide to head indoors.
Under the concrete angel Bottom's wing
are four tiny, baby bird feathers.

My husband must have found them while mowing
or picking up windfalls. One apple fell while I sat
forming a perfect triangle. Positive signs?

I pick up the feather-lets to place in my feather jar.
They are beside me as I type. Will my concerns uplift?
How much weight of the world can I take on? Float?

Dandelion Wishes

She has dandelion wishes and lioness dreams. J. Iron Word

Edna St. Vincent Millay thought our life can be as beautiful
as a dandelion.

Carl Sagan suggests the ship of imagination, as organic
as a dandelion, will carry us to worlds of dreams and facts.

Andrew Mason says if dandelions were hard to grow they
would be most welcome in any lawn.

When we see dandelions we see weeds or wishes.
I see wishes. Women's wishes have been weeded too long.

Unlike the lazy lions, the lioness takes care of things.
Men have let the planet down. Time for women's wishes.

Dandelions are a symbol of persistence in the face
of difficulty. We need dandelion dreamers.

Perhaps we should weed thoughts of weedy people?
If we do not dream and act we may all perish.

Already the dandelions are changed into vanishing ghosts. Celia Thaxter

Dandelion Scuffles

The bright yellow that means rebirth instead of destruction. The promise that life can go on, no matter how bad our losses. That it can be good again. Suzanne Collins

The leggy dandelions tower over the grass
and many garden plants. Some are about
three feet tall. Ones near the patio–about a foot.

My husband picked three puffballs and dumped
them in the compost. He dug out the front yard
mower survivors. We are not watering this summer.

I scolded him to leave my backyard companions
alone and let them lurch toward sun. I have
about seven left which I hope he does not pull.

It is an on-going battle. I'm a dandelion defender.
He is such an environmentalist in most ways.
He uses a hand mower. He supports green causes.

I applaud my defiant dandelions. I'm not a weeder.
He revels in the sunflower towers he grew from seed.
We agree on these yellow blooms. Why is only one a weed?

After over a half-century of marriage, there are
some unresolved issues. Dandelions is one.
Why can't he put dandelions on salad at least?

Maybe brew some dandelion tea or wine? I just do not
like their unnatural death and trashing them on compost.
At least they will enrich the earth and may even grow again.

But it is the attitude and lack of respect shown them
that upsets me. As I bask in their temporary glow,
I want them to know I am their champion.

The man who worries morning and night about the dandelions in the lawn will find relief in loving the dandelions. Liberty Hyde Bailey

Six Feathers

While picking up windfall apples,
my husband found six feathers
in our backyard lawn.

He knew I collected found feathers,
so he anchored them under the angel
Bottom's concrete feet on the blue table.

I do not venture on uneven ground,
so the feathers I find are found near
the patio grass edge.

Four feathers have blue on one side-
probably Stellar jays. A smaller brownish-gray
feather could be from an unnamed-to-me bird.

The largest feather is a true mystery. Almost
quill-size it has gray and black stripes, a touch
of white down its spine.

I noticed he did not pluck the dandelions
in the grass or garden. He even left
a puffball undisturbed, after my complaints.

A butterfly landed briefly on a new dandelion.
Another butterfly just flew by. Several birds
of diverse markings and sizes snack, full-feathered.

The protected sunflower turned its puffed out head
from the neighbor's new shed which just misses
the lowest power line by barely a foot.

I take the feathers inside for my feather jar.
I consider it an atonement gift to me for his slaughter
of dandelions–detente from our dandelion disagreement.

Since he did not disturb the current batches, perhaps
he is letting the backyard run wild, for a while. For now
he is feathering his nest for my favor.

Hope is a Thing with Feathers

Hope is a thing with feathers that perches in the soul. Emily Dickinson

Around ten, I move my backyard chair to reflect.
I place it mid-yard out of the shadow of a hazelnut tree,
my back to sun, shade my face.

Near my feet I see a mid-sized jay feather, larger
than the baby fluffy feathers gifted to me by my
husband, placed under an angel's concrete wing yesterday.

Blue on one edge, gray on the other—
about the length of my mid-finger.
I pick it up for my feather jar.

Emily Dickinson's poem comes to mind
as I twiddle the feather in my fingers.
My soul could use some hope.

I deep-breathe my breaths of fire,
imagine spinning my chakras with chi,
try to lift and free my concerns to the air.

Two apples plop nearby to join
the pimpled lawn. Above me a stellar jay
chirps and tussles with pesky nuts.

A few green-husked hazelnuts plunk
to the ground. When the husks tan, they open
like wings in the littered grass.

There is a flourish of chattering jays
in the apple and hazelnut canopies
knocking down nuts and windfalls.

The sun penetrates my back and warms me.
The wind chimes tinkle in gentle breezes.
Perhaps today will be more hopeful than I thought.

I carry the found feather, tightly into the house.
I pat the head of feather-free, cherub angel,
named Bottom. I hold my own feathered hope.

Orchard Overseer

Our orchard production is unbalanced.
The two apple and two hazelnut trees
pop and plunk all over the backyard.

The plums were modestly few,
pears more abundant, but the one
peach will not make me a peacherino.

Since I do not eat any of the fruit
or nuts, I leave pick up to hubby
or birds. Perhaps some squirrels.

The deer are barred admittance due
to their proclivity to Lyme disease tics,
ugly warts, fleas and scat donations.

Raccoons chew a few windfalls.
Nutria and rabbits seem to have
found other feeding grounds.

I watch the bees, bugs and butterflies
dip and sip, content to let them dine.
I miss the chopped down cherry tree.

After years of contention with birds,
we finally just shared the organic cherries.
Then disease struck, leading to its demise.

We do have strawberries, blueberries,
some raspberries. I only eat the blueberries
and pick none of them– just enjoy them.

So I am a passive observer, not much
of a consumer. I appreciate the colors
and textures. I tend to let them freely be.

The Gleaner

My husband cherishes every apple
our two trees produce. He finds a use
for each either picked or windfalls.

Most of the apples are out of reach,
hidden in the canopies awaiting
winds to loosen their grips.

If they are wormy or scaly,
he cuts the blemish out or
donates them to pigs or horses.

Those he does not give away,
he wraps in newspapers
to store for months in his shed.

Some windfalls get baked in sun
and smooshy. They get composted.
Some wild creatures get there first.

But most windfalls bruise before
picked up. If other animals do not
eat them, he will dig out the brown spots.

As the apples bubble the lawn
in diverse patterns, some geometric,
I ponder their conditions, their destinies.

Some apples are really red before downfall.
The first windfalls were very green.
The crop is thinning. Harvest dwindling.

The days I sit in the backyard to huff
breaths of fire, balance chakras, slurp chi,
I wonder will they be cider, pie, snack?

The gleaner piles chunks on cereal.
I am a watcher, not diner of apples.
Apple-pickers, windfall- recyclers...kudos.

Building a Shed

Our side neighbor is building a wooden shed
in the back corner of our property line.
One side will serve as fence.

The carpenters' hammers bang, rat-a--tat-tats
from their nail and staple guns. The sunflower
turns its head away from the noise.

All the plants can't uproot and leave
for quieter clime. The dandelions
remain upright, tilt toward sun.

I sit on my blue pillow tranquilly
trying to absorb some chi
and balance my spinning chakras.

Oregon recently encouraged building
backyard small dwellings to house
more people per lot. In-filling.

Perhaps our dream of building a tiny house
is now feasible. Our shed would not interfere.
It hugs the house under the roof-line.

Yesterday our neighbors' old metal shed
clanked to the ground, pounded to carry
away for the new structure.

Today machine and hand tools disrupt
the calm, jar the nerves. The news
is unhinging enough. I go indoors.

Inside the murmur from building is still
heard, if dulled a tad. This is temporary.
If only the bad news was transitory.

Warming Up

Around two I venture into the backyard
to commune with nature, despite the warning
it could be up into the 90's this afternoon.

The gentle breeze tingles jingles
in the wind chimes and spins the pinwheel.
In the shade I am very comfortable.

The solid roof-line shadow merges
with the lacy canopy shade, which
covers much of the summery yard.

One obstinate sunflower refuses
to face the sun, as the others
glare and glow in sun-rays.

Hidden birds squawk in different
bird-languages. I only see one
stellar jay flitting about like a butterfly.

Perhaps the jay thinks I am wearing
all blue in solidarity. The nut pecking
and tugging carries on, oblivious of me.

Several butterflies make a pass-by
but do not choose to land. I consider
it a greeting from other dimensions.

Windfall apples could bake. Dry leaves
and hazelnut husks could crisp and re-shape
in their fallen, arid condition. They turn brown.

A siren wails. Hopefully someone gets
help. My gold crown fell off at lunch.
My appointment is tomorrow. I'll eat gingerly.

The warmth is welcome. I am rarely as warm
as my colleagues. They put on fans and I
put on sweatshirts. Today just a tee shirt.

I am reluctant to go inside to air-conditioning.
My husband tucked two feathers under the feet
of a concrete angel. One gray. A bird-crone like me?

Beat the Heat

This afternoon it could reach 100 degrees,
so to beat the heat I retreat to the backyard
late morning, to stir my chakras and inhale chi.

Two apple and two hazelnut canopies
interlace to provide mid-yard shade,
light-spots speckle the grass.

In the notch of a hazelnut tree,
a stellar jay perches, then climbs
to the first branch, searching for nuts.

Shiny blue back skirmishes among the leaves,
pecking at hazelnut husks, until they fall.
Wings flare and beak squawks.

En route to the other hazelnut tree,
the jay leaps on an apple bough
plunking down an apple bird-fall.

The ritual continues, screeching
and pecking until a husk falls. Then
the jay wanders the ground, searching.

Apparently the shadow obscures
the winged-out husks nestled
in the grass with the apple windfalls.

Finally the beak clutches the nut
to poke at under the blueberry bush.
Other jays flutter about with butterflies.

Seven sunflowers boldly face the sun,
not crouching in shade like the jays.
Butterflies give the sunflowers a fly-by.

I have beaten the heat. I watch the industrious
winged-ones and decide on sunflower mode,
and soak in the perfect temperature rays.

Labor Day Weekend Monday

Around three, the creatures and features
in our backyard are not working much.
Bees, birds, and bugs are on siesta.

The limp breezes do not budge the weathervane
and only occasionally give the pinwheel
a whirl or whimper a wind chime.

Tree-shadows dance over the un-watered,
scraggly unmown lawn in wind-gusts.
My back and shoulders soak in the sun's warmth.

Gawky, giant sunflower stalks' bow
thick heads, appear to be nodding off.
A motionless green hose traverses grass.

The windfall apples await pickup, baking
in the sun. One more apple plops.
No nut fans to probe fallen filberts.

Two butterflies criss-cross the lawn and
garden, fly erratically without landing. They're
the only active ones in the backyard.

I huff breaths of fire to enervate my chakras,
try to connect Earth's core to cosmos. That
is the intention, but no guarantees I succeed.

I sit, wearing my husband's shoes, since I can't
go barefoot in the backyard. I am shoeless
inside due to a swollen foot from a fall.

So sluggish me is no one to point fingers
at others here who appear to just relax
and enjoy the simmering, summer day.

My own shoes pinch my ballooned foot.
I appreciate these larger borrowed boats.
I'll sail inside, become shoeless and moodle.

Almost Autumn

Autumn (sorry Rilke, you got it wrong), Fall is not the harbinger of death and death is not the end of life to those who believe that we are the stuff of starlight. Mary Daniels

In almost autumn, (official in a few weeks)
the backyard still resists the grip of fall.
The seasonal transition still serotinal.

Ten sunflowers, tall and majestic
bob in the breeze and radiate like sun
on this lovely clear, almost cloudless day.

The windfalls plop at an astonishing rate.
Apples still ripening on the bending boughs.
More hazelnuts on the branch, than husks on ground.

Yes, some leaves have fallen, tanned and crisped.
But the canopies camouflage hacked spruce
and lopsided fruit and nut trees.

The sunflowers totally hide the weathervane.
Tootsie angel's horn. She tells us where
the wind blows. Seems she's stuck toward west.

The rusty angel Airlika hanging from a hazelnut
limb does not sway in this limp wind. Windchimes
barely tingle or jingle. Indecisive butterfly flits.

As for death, in any season, if we are starlight
or stardust, we go with the flow to the next
adventure in consciousness or form.

Nature has its rhythms and cycles like we do.
I see the backyard change its role in the seasons.
I just hope people keep Gaia viable and sustainable.

Fall and Spring are motions. Both harbingers
of the next transformations. Summer and winter
are not as obvious in their names for purpose.

Today I absorb the warmth and glow. I enjoy
this season. I have decorated for Halloween,
especially love crone witches with hooked noses.

Fall is not all fallen and death. Perhaps we can
peek beyond the veil, harvest and wonder at
the mystery of life whenever the grim reaper appears.

Cosmic Messages

Once you have freed yourself, even momentarily, from the distraction of the outer world and all its drama and chaos...this is the place where the universe can reach you.
  Sara Wiseman

At eleven when I go to the backyard
to probe and ponder cosmic conundrums,
it is cloudy with intermittent shadows.

The lawn has an acute case of apple acne—
bumpy windfalls, red, ripe, ready to pick.
No evidence creatures have chewed them.

Bees, bugs and birds seem to be taking
a siesta elsewhere. Five lonely sunflowers
splay their petals with a droop.

Huddled in an afghan from the chilly breeze,
I try to focus on receiving cosmic messages,
as shadows wax and wane beneath the canopies.

Supposedly, messages come when relaxed in nature,
reading, listening to music, journaling, without attachment
to any particular idea–how it should or should not be.

I am not skilled at detaching and stillness in any
mode, but the backyard seems as good a place
as any. So I deep breathe to spin some chakras.

Sara suggests to listen for "sweet whispers
of the universe" to simply begin. I tend to
think angel numbers and finding feathers,

are indications some otherworldly being
is trying to indicate they have my back
or I am on the right track.

But how wonderful to think I might hear
or see another realm in this dimension
and not just in dreams! Worth a try?

At my feet green husks of hazelnuts
with green nuts, tossed by birds from branches
uneaten, left to ripen or rot.

I sit and shiver wondering what I can ground.
Will a thought emanate from some cosmic connection?
I wait, observe what's fallen around me.

Awash with Mushrooms

Every day I peek or sit in the backyard
more mushrooms appear.
From the pebbles between patio bricks,
arcing around the hazelnut tree
facing East and touching garden wall–
an explosion of mushrooms.

The oldest ones have flattened
and browned with crumpled edges.
The newest ones are white
with sprinkles like spices.
The progression arrays
like a mushroom rainbow.

Drooping from the garden
are the heavy heads of sunflowers,
bending almost to the ground.
Dowager humps of their aging.
But like the mushrooms, they burst
forth with sunny glow-light.

Soon my floral companions
will join the diminishing windfalls
of apples and pears, leave the scene.
I will miss the ardent sunflowers
whose daily expansions delighted me.
From seeds to cascades, light-flows.

Why I am so intrigued with quirky mushrooms?
I am not sure. Do I still yearn for fairies
using them as umbrellas, center of dance circles?
Do they stir imagination? Focus attention on aging?
From great beauty to crushed ugliness, I guess
I think of what we are doing to Gaia and sadden.

On October First

Fall puts on a showy preview.
This morning three turkeys walked down the street.
I have seen deer stroll down the road, but
squirrels, raccoons, birds, hide behind curtains.
In our backyard today the sun spotlights bowing sunflowers.
Shriveling, droopy sunflower heads go to seed.
A speckled arc of mushrooms bends around the hazelnut tree.
A windfall apple smashed a burgeoning brown mushroom.
Apples and pears bubble beneath thinning canopies.
My new enameled tin stellar jay perches beside me
as I inhale chi, balance my chakras, absorb chilly sun.

As I inhale chi, balance my chakras, absorb chilly sun,
my new enameled tin stellar jay perches beside me.
Apples and pears bubble beneath thinning canopies.
A windfall apple smashed a burgeoning mushroom.
A speckled arc of mushrooms bends around the hazelnut tree.
Shriveling, droopy sunflower heads go to seed.
In our backyard today the sun spotlights bowing sunflowers.
Squirrels, raccoons, birds hide behind curtains.
I have seen deer stroll down the road but,
this morning three wild turkeys walked down the street.
Fall puts on a showy preview.

Waves of Nature

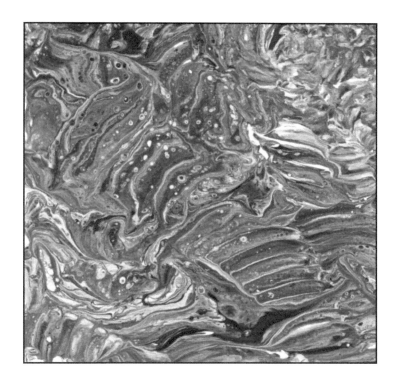

We can speak without voice
to the trees and the clouds
and the waves of the sea.
Without words they respond
through the rustling of leaves
and the moving of clouds
and the murmuring of the sea.

Paul Tillich

Balancing in the Backyard

On a late afternoon in June, I commune
with chi, breathe deeply in my chair,
darkled by roof-line shade.

The sun winks with the clouds,
blinks shadows across the lawn.
Recent rain refreshed the dry yard.

A patch of white clover rings the stump
of the chopped cherry tree. A cluster
of yellow clover in a hollow escaped the mower.

A green hose traverses the grass, splitting
the lawn. Wind wrangles wind chimes
and spins the blurring pinwheel.

The sunflowers inch upward, growing taller,
soon to bloom above the miniature red roses
and ripening strawberries below.

The apples are beginning to bulge. I can't see
the progress of peaches, pears and plums.
Leaves camouflage any hazelnut upstarts.

A skirmish between birds in the bushes–they
squark and rustle the branches. An incessant
nearby alarm monotonously buzzes for minutes.

The interruptions cease and quiet returns.
I envision a column of white light and huff
and puff breaths of fire to balance chakras.

Before I go inside, I change the prone position
of concrete angel, Bottom, on blue table
so he can get a new viewpoint to ponder.

Follow the Hose

After a sun-soaked weekend,
I returned to the backyard to inhale chi.
A green hose snakes to the garden.

We no longer water the lawn, waiting
for fall rains to revive the desiccated grass.
It still has some green whiskers. Fewer weeds.

The white clover withered beige, only
three dandelions. Yellow clover mostly gone.
The lawn will be mowed in one day.

Some smart dandelions followed the hose
to the watered garden area. The sunflowers
grow with gusto. Blueberries beg to be picked.

There is a patch of three orange blossoms,
whose name I have forgotten. Canopy shadows
link across the lawn. Apples ripen, some fall.

My husband is Johnny-on-the-spot to pick up
windfalls before they rot. He protects the crop
for eaters. Even shares with horses, other critters.

But my eye goes where the hose goes. There
water encourages two peaches, plums, pears
and other floral varieties. The lawn looks bland.

The fruit is abundant, water-filled. Below the wall
the thirsty yard awaits mower, drop-outs, the beige
cones like spruce poops. Compost marinates.

After a weekend immersed in art displays and
science exhibits, I'm back to see nature perform.
A few birds and butterflies look as well.

Yellow Patches

Our first out of reach peach on
top of a scraggly, struggling tree,
a globe of yellow in sparse green.

At its feet are three dandelions
in the garden out of mower's way.
Soon sunflowers will stretch and bloom.

Yellow clover remnants hug the ground.
The white variety like ghosts surround
the stump of the chopped cherry tree.

Some unripe windfall apples have a tinge
of yellow, but not radiant, more beige.
The cling-ons are ripening abundantly.

The sun hides behind the clouds,
provides no shade or shadows.
I treasure all yellow in the yard.

As I sit and try to still, download chi,
I do not feel my higher self descending
in me–but I protect dandelions, cherish yellow.

The Puny Peach

The last puny peach plopped
and was chewed by some critter,
who just nibbled and left it.

My husband hoped he could pick
the last peach before it fell, but
the unripe, tiny peach bailed.

Since we only had two peaches
on an ailing organic host, he did
not get to pick either peach to eat.

Windfall apples pimple the lawn,
get plunked into white buckets.
Some are scaly and wormy.

My husband tries to find mouths
for them all. He will cut out the rot
spots and munch away.

We share plums and pears as well as
peaches and apples. Strawberries and
blueberries also. We try to be sustainable.

A lone dandelion puffball awaits
a wind-wave good-bye. A butterfly
flits across lawn, but does not land.

Suddenly about six feet beside me
a hummingbird pauses in midair to stare
at me. Without missing a beat,

the hummingbird moves in front of me,
pauses again, glistening in the sun, then
flies out of the yard without landing.

I wonder if there is a message from those
beings that fly and do not land and those
that fall and do? Wings suggest hope?

But a fallen peach says things are not peachy?
Rotten apples question our core values? What
does a close encounter with a hummingbird mean?

Transitions

Tomorrow will be July first.
We are transitioning into summer—
Oregon's dry, warm, sunny summers.

Wildfire smoke is on the horizon.
But for now the seasonal passage
greens and flourishes.

I sit in the backyard to inhale chi
and hopefully energy and exhale
to spin my lazy chakras.

Two fuzzy contrails drift east,
floating closer together until
diffusing out of sight beyond trees.

Apples plump, increase their diameter
and blush. Much like my apple belly
and embarrassment.

Stellar jays squat on bark dust, probe— then
fly to nearby bushes. When they are still
upon the ground, I wonder their intentions.

Butterflies flit fly and land, short flights
without purpose or direction it seems,
whereas a fly buzzes my head.

The tinkling of wind chimes and slow
whir of the pinwheel calm
my restless spirit and soul.

I look at the grimy concrete angel
on a dirty, crusty blue table. Soon he will
be cleansed and painted in silver glitter.

He will glisten near rusty angel Airlika,
and gray, plain weathervane, Tootsie.
A trio of angels bringing light to darkness.

Tranquility

On a cloudless, warm summer day,
I sit on my chair in the backyard
trying to absorb some chi.

I breathe deeply, huff to ruffle
my chakras into balance. Relax
my achy body in the shade.

Canopy shadows mottle the grass.
Leaves rustle. My eyes follow a butterfly.
We survey the burgeoning backyard.

A lone peach perches precariously,
high above the rock wall, too high to reach.
When it falls, it will be a hard landing.

A stellar jay skirmishes in the underbrush,
hobbles to bark dust and plops. I think
the jay is dead, sunbathes or splatters.

But the bird revives and returns
to the bushes. A brisk breeze spins
the pinwheel, jingles the wind chimes.

From this angle it appears a sunflower
bloom is tickling the belly of the weathervane
angel. Tootsie is stuck facing west.

I cannot see the pears or plums, but
reports are they are dropping fruit
for pick up. The apples are into overdrive.

A branch broke from their weight. Downfalls
and windfalls are mostly small and unripe.
But bucketfuls are forthcoming.

The yard is quiet, just murmuring and simmering.
I bask in its warmth and try to sponge
its tranquility, release my anxiety.

If I Go Outside Today

If I go outside today,
I'd better get on my way,
clouds gather thick and gray.

If I go outside today,
I'll grab my jacket and sachet
to my chi-chair and mind-play.

When I go outside today,
for a backyard survey,
abundant weeds on display.

When I go outside today
I spot a solo stellar jay,
on the fence looking for prey.

When I go outside today
I see an errant sunray
spill shadows–storm delay?

When I go outside today,
gusts push pinwheel, limbs sway
and wind chimes wrestle but obey.

When I go outside today,
my thoughts tend to runaway.
I worry for world to be okay.

When I go outside today.
I shiver, try to waylay
fears and dismay.

When I go outside today
I witness the backyard's bouquet
and burgeoning fruit buffet.

When I go outside today
I'm uplifted by this foray,
take a brief respite, holiday.

When I go inside today
I hope progress will prevail, outweigh
the misguided citizens of our Milky way.

Everywhen
   all the time. always. Dictionary.com

Jubiliantly, I walk to the backyard to intake chi.
The USA Women's soccer team won the World Cup
over the Netherlands. Both teams have women coaches.
         May empowered women shine everywhere, everywhen.

A tangled hose waters the strawberry patch
beneath a batch of blueberries on flourishing
bushes. Some tiny apples plopped before their prime.
         May berries and fruit be fruitful everywhen.

Sunflowers tower over small roses. Roses
observe strawberries ripening below. Azaleas,
rhododendrons and other flowers await their season.
         May flowers bloom everywhen.

Ants traverse grass blades guided by their GPS.
Bees, bugs of every kind seek sustenance.
Flies flash before my eyes. Butterflies flutter.
         May these buggy things remain everywhen.

On blue table, Bottom, the newly shiny- covered angel,
takes it easy while Airlika on a hazelnut limb and Tootsie
on her weathervane, toot their silent horns.
         May angels of all kinds protect us everywhen.

A few buds of white clover and two of yellow survive
the mower with a dandelion huddled near the rock wall.
I miss their fallen comrades, mown down to rise again.
         May weeds prevail everywhen.

Stellar jays flit limb to limb, ground where other
creatures prey. Intricate interactions to watch
in fascination and wonder. Part of All.
         May winged ones and groundlings play their roles everywhen.

I propose a weed patch. A safe haven where their colors
can bloom. Just as other flora have their patches,
why do we discriminate against weeds?
         May wildness and nature have their niches, everywhen.

As I celebrate diversity and perseverance, I hope humanity's
impacts on the environment improve as climate change
advances. Let's increase our chances of survival.
         May positive actions win everywhen.

Re-Visioning

The shadow-less lawn dulls and lulls
in the backyard under overcast skies.
Even the breeze doesn't make leaf-waves.

Occasional soft wind-chimes riffs, but stiff
pinwheel does not budge. The hose droops
over the rock wall, leaves long imprint in grass.

A stellar jay, not partridge, in our pear tree.
One brief leap to the peach top, then
heads to the limb-whacked tall spruce.

I am grateful the dense foliage of the hazelnut
tree conceals the acne on the spruce trunk–
the blunt wounds of artless arborists.

Come winter I'll wish I built a treehouse on it
like the tea house on Treehouse Masters,
restoring beauty to a similarly abused tree.

Sunflowers seem to inch daily toward
flowering. Butterfly took cover today
from the approaching storm.

The white and yellow clover hover
in their domains. If we have blueberries
and strawberries they hide from me.

Our neighbor yells "Ow!" as he dumps
his wheelbarrow. No other mammals
around to offer comfort or calm.

I prefer sun when I sit to draw chi
and wind to twirl my chakras. Also not
as chilly. Today the yard appears static.

I carry a glass of water and a brownie inside.
Chocolate enlivens everything and shifts moods.
Tomorrow will the backyard appear brighter?

Chasing Earth Ecstasies

The mind will tell you one thing or the other: what you don't have, what you think you need, why this isn't good, why that isn't enough. Sara Wiseman

It is ecstasy to become aware of this life!
But becoming aware opens you to what's not working.
Beside joy, there is plenty of strife—
heart- rending, mind-boggling, knee-jerking.
It is hard to find ecstasy in any individual.
Is ecstasy available to us all?

This nectar of the sky, the winds, the air
is increasingly marred, scarred, polluted.
Youth's view of the future brings despair.
Their climate change advocacy is to be saluted.
We need more than cap and trade.
We need pollution to completely fade.

This ecstasy of the earth, the plants, the stones!
When well-tended and sustained,
such beauty graces all species' homes.
For eons Gaia has been maintained.
When habitats are damaged and destroyed,
restorers and nurturers must be employed.

This grand expanse of earth: all of it and all it contains!
We are to steward, not exploit. All's bequeathed in cosmic trust.
The responsibility for all life mostly remains
in our consciousness. Protect best we can–a must.
We are part of a multiverse.
The eyesore of this universe?

Created by Light, for your immersion and your enjoyment.
This assumption may not be true.
What about our impact on all life meant
to share this existence with you?
How can your presence be an asset?
What ground rules do we tend to forget?

Created by Light, so you as Light can be here and feel it.
Perhaps it is not all about you and how you feel?
If light perhaps you came to heal it?
Perhaps you were lured by Earth's appeal?
Getting here you came to the conclusion
life on Gaia could be an illusion?

Crop Circles

Celestial tattoos or human hoaxes, mysterious
patterns appear in cereal grain fields around
the world, stirring curiosity about who made them.

Aliens, time travelers, humans, energy sources
from space or vortexes within the Earth?
"Cerealogists" research possible theories.

Complex math, sacred geometry, cosmic
messages have been decoded. Often magnificent
circles and other geometric designs magically appear...

If nothing else, this public art–often formed near
highways and at night delights the curious.
Space craft and light orbs have been reported.

I look at the intricate patterns and marvel
at the artists wherever they came from.
They stir my imagination.

When I look at my monotonous, blunt-cut lawn,
no wonder I love colorful weeds to spruce it up.
Maybe I could plant grains, braid and pattern it?

Could I find images to stamp? Crop Circles
leave imprints after mowed. I'd have faint
etchings after balding the strands.

The flat palette is just perfect for art. Around
the edges, flowers and, walls could frame the art.
Our inanimate, wild yard animals edge a gallery.

My husband hand-mows. Why can't he mow
a design? Maybe a labyrinth following an imprint
or creating new ones. Just think the beauty!

When I go to the backyard to chi-gather or
passers-by see our yard galleries we can
ponder the mystery and surprises of Gaia.

I can dream a cosmic tattoo artist brings me
a sign. I would get binary code translated, as
visionaries have, to share with us all.

Greenland

Greenland has gone from ten months
of winter to five months in a few decades.
The glaciers melt with astonishing speed.

Greenland has 0% arable land and their marine
life style is challenged with the rapid changes.
Ocean levels are rising. Icebergs drift by.

Adding to the problems is Trump wanting
to buy Greenland from Denmark. It is not
for sale, of course. Only Trump would think so.

Greenland is at the vanguard of climate change
and impacts coastlines globally. The poles
are melting. Other places face drought.

With migrations of millions moving north
to escape climate conditions, we have
just begun to cope, or not, with this situation.

Greenland and other polar regions are
facing these changes now, helpless
as glaciers calve and water encroaches.

Pollution of land, water and air, plastic
waste dumping, wildlife species going extinct...
We are bombarded. Some solutions exist.

Perhaps Greenland can show a way to deal?
As world-wide youth march and fight for a future,
they may claim ice-freed polar lands to survive?

Whatever happens, Greenland is becoming
a truly green land, perhaps more habitable?
Poor Greenland, what would more settlements bring?

Scientists have found ways to adapt, but political
inertia, denial and greed prevail. Some projects
offer hope, but enough in time?

Hopefully the media attention on Greenland
is fleeting and they can adapt in peace and
with urgency, a beacon for what is possible.

Riding the Wild Waves

But where, after all, would be the poetry of the sea were there no wild waves.
Joshua Slocum

If the sea is a metaphor for life,
poetry can create wild waves.
If it is for peak experiences and strife,
let's hope a tsunami behaves.
       The wild world has become tame.
       A plasticized ocean puts us to shame.

Poetry can create wild waves,
freeing words to create.
Different expressions bring raves.
Many poems to appreciate.
       We surf waves with some skill.
       Some drown and some thrill.

If it is for peak experiences and strife,
riding the waves is a roller-coaster,
until the end of the rife.
Some are whiners, some are boasters
       But as long as we ride,
       we hope luck is on our side.

Let's hope a tsunami behaves
and we are far enough back on shore.
We can explore the depths of caves,
not hear the ocean's roar?
       We hope for understanding,
       wherever we are landing.

The wild world has become tame,
but we are losing our control.
Plenty of us are to blame.
Much destruction to patrol.
       So much of the planet is in danger.
       Not enough of us to be a changer?

A plasticized ocean puts is to shame,
clogging, killing sea creatures.
We ride future waves with no claim
on how to sustain Gaia's features.
       I'm riding the waves–seasick.
       How does this reality tick?

Keep Birds Flying

*North America's skies are lonelier and quieter as nearly 3 billion fewer birds
soar in the air than in 1970... the bird population in the United States and
Canada was probably around 10.1 billion nearly a century ago and has fallen to
about 7.2 billion birds.* Seth Borenstein and Christina Larson

Weather radar tracks bird flights,
      provides data on migrating birds,
            follows trends for 529 species.

Birds eat bugs that destroy food plants
      and carry encephalitis. Sparrows
            were at the top of the loss list.

Eastern meadowlarks are down three-quarters,
      western meadowlarks nearly as hard hit.
            Bobwhite quail are down 80%.

Grassland birds are less than half of what
      they used to be. But bluebirds are increasing.
            People tend to prop them up.

Birds decline because of habitat loss,
      cats and windows. Stop using pesticides
            and buy forest-like farm coffee.

As people pay more attention to the climate,
      perhaps they will protect birds, treat
            windows and keep cats indoors.

Birds fly in polluted air, land on infected soil,
      eat lethal bugs. My backyard birds
            dine organically, but cats stray in.

The Shining Web

A dew-diamond-studded web
dangled from the bottom
of the handicapped parking sign.

The sun was just right to highlight
each connection for a gleaming
necklace. I paused and smiled.

After an hour of grunting and groaning
in my exercise class, I dragged out
the door, clasping my walker

As I was getting into my blue Fit,
I hoped to be cheered by the sparking
spider-gem. I looked up at the sign.

The light had shifted, the web grayed
and frayed, as if the wind had a tantrum
or something had an issue with the web.

I took down my permit from the window.
The once beautiful web was torn apart.
Where was the weaver? Her effort unraveled.

I could think of many metaphors
for this changing situation. My sense
of sadness, made me delay leaving.

As I drove away, I vowed to remember
the dazzle, bright beauty of the web
and wear it over my heart.

Autumnal Farewells

Today is the first official autumn day
I sit in the backyard to gather chi
and survey transitions into fall.

A few stray dandelions sun-dot grass.
Sunflowers droop heads west on arched
stalks, still camouflage angel weathervane.

Beige-tinged pears sprawl in garden,
really past golden ripeness,
an abundant crop this year.

Windfall red apples still pop in lawn,
await pick up. Apples on lower boughs
cling for a few more days unless plucked.

Mushroom colonies expand in front
and backyards. The largest batch is
in patio gravel and at patio's grass edge.

In two days, they have mushroomed
from 23 to 33–all sizes and clusters.
One is a flattening, browning pancake.

Under the hazelnut tree is another grouping,
growing daily as well. I've asked the mower
to preserve the closest colony to me.

I want to watch its process–growth to decay,
how the shape transforms and changes color.
Like sculptures they are molded uniquely.

Beside me on the blue table are three feathers
my husband found for me during windfalls pick-ups
and before the next mowing. Two are blue.

There are no birds in the yard at eleven.
Only sound is muted wind chimes.
I clutch the feathers and go inside.

The yard will become more and more barren.
Flowers fade. Fruit harvested. Birds fly away.
I mourn the ending diversity and warmth.

Quotidian Waves

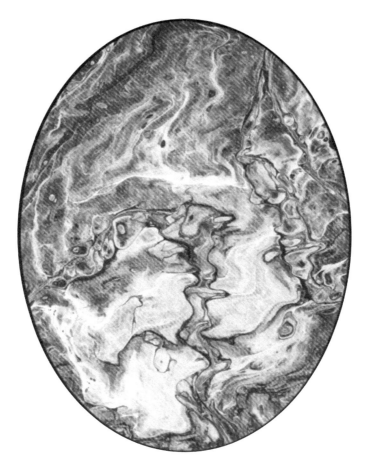

You must live in the present,
launch yourself in every wave,
find your eternity
in each moment.

Henry David Thoreau

Just-Summer

Yellow and red roses, honeysuckle
drape over the wooden fence
beside the driveway.

In the front yard patches of pink,
perhaps clover, rim the concrete
chunk wall, avoid the mower.

Summer has just begun, so
they can sun-dose before
the heat waves start.

In the backyard yellow "star"
clover sprinkle in clusters,
sun-dots amid the grass.

The triangular niche in the rock wall holds
eight sunflower plants stretching above
a mini-red rose plant and unripe strawberries.

Blue-tinged birds glide under a contrail
scarred sky, stripe fading in blue air
with striated, thin clouds.

My first day returning to exercise class
after weeks of travel and congestion.
Baskets full of tissues emptied.

My glasses frame arrived. They no longer
leap over my left ear and require
an eye-lace to remain in place.

I started a file for a new poetry book
where this poem will go. In just-summer
I hope to jumpstart spring-sapped energy.

I gather chi in shade for the first time
outside this season in short-sleeves.
My Derek Hough tee-shirt dances.

Exiting Exercise Class

Heading for the exit door,
gleaming equipment shines.
Sweaty athletes strain.

Their abs and muscles glisten
and pop from their bones,
ripple down their bodies.

They are the A team.
The seniors' B-team class
passes by. I am barely B team.

My bulges are butt, boobs
and belly, as I push my walker
by their sleek machines.

They try not to groan. Some pause,
smile or greet me. Most are intent
on their self-aggrandizement.

I look for the geezer with the long, thick,
white ponytail. I am envious of his
flowing hair, not his bulk. He's not here.

My thin, short hair limps. I drag my hulk.
Since I exercised seated, I do not sweat
much, more wilt. My jaw– word pincers

Outside the door, I do not look back. I look
forward to sitting at my computer with
unsweetened iced tea and dark chocolate.

Blueberry Pickers

Grandpa and grandson bolt to the backyard
          to pick organic blueberries
                    from an abundantly endowed bush.

They carry recycled plastic containers
          to hold their harvest. Grandpa
                    re-purposes them for many uses.

He washes the containers and air-dries them
          on the top of the refrigerator. They tumble.
                    He puts them back to new re-uses.

He fills them with berries and nuts from his garden,
          loose items from the natural food coop.
                    The nuggets bubble in the fridge.

The pickers return with heaping blueberries.
          They find tops so James' crop does not spill
                    when he drives home.

Their outer layer is rain-sprinkled.
          James puts his sweatshirt in the dryer.
                    He rounds up his treasures to leave.

He never fails to tell us he loves us. We echo.
          My love-waves waft to follow him
                    whenever and wherever he goes.

Overcast

On an overcast afternoon, I go to the backyard
to perk my chakras and calm my mind.
No shadows lace the lawn.

A few stalks and blades give the mower the finger.
No water runs through the loopy hose.
Weathervane and wind chimes static.

There is a dark scar in the grass where dirt
was added to cover the protruding root
of the mangled blue spruce.

A jittery butterfly flits with brief landings.
A darkened bird flies above concealing
its identifiable colors. No sound.

The yard seems unsettled. Aborted applets
fall before reaching full term. Overladen limbs
droop from apple overloads' growing girth.

Things seem stagnant or unsatisfying.
Blurs of color. Hacked blooms
I applaud the few wily weeds.

I skip the negative headlines in the newspapers
as much as I can. I avoid the boisterous TV
news. I need renewal and refreshing.

I loved the sparkle of Macy's fireworks,
the songs and dance by Derek Hough.
The USA women soccer players shine no. 1.

But then there are the aftermaths. The smoke
smogging the sky from fireworks. The unequal
pay and treatment of women in sports–everywhere.

In my hermitage I cannot escape the turbulence
surrounding the planet. I go inside to change
my point of view and attitude. I can't.

Making Waves

Theme for 2019 Da Vinci Days Celebration of Art, Science and Technology
Corvallis, Oregon   July 19-21

On a sunny, warm Saturday afternoon,
we headed to the fairgrounds to meet
our daughter and son-in-law.

I wore a 2006 DaVinci t-shirt and baseball hat,
slathered sun screen and we were off. Slowly
it is coming back after a few years hiatus.

The big attraction is the Kinetic Sculptures—
this year for adults and kids. They parade,
brave sand hill, float the river, slosh mud pit.

Pedal-powered, artistic vehicles, crews perform a
comic song and hand out colorful cards. All
relate to the theme: Making Waves. Themed costumes.

Local organizations had information booths,
Oregon State and Linn-Benton Community College
had many science exhibits. An electric car show.

Arts and Crafts were in another area.
A player of a Spiderharp and light guitar
was fascinating. They have other performers.

I bought a blue bowl to support the Hungry Bowl
organization which gives funds to food banks.
Bowls are donated by local students of ceramics.

We were able to eat in an area near the stage
where crews of the kinetic sculptures sang
and danced original songs to their vehicle.

They have activities for kids, a rad robot
(Man inside), many interactive exhibits.
Lots to learn. Volunteers wore blue tees.

In DaVinci Days glory days it sprawled on
OSU campus, downtown park and fairgrounds.
The leadership floundered and sponsors lost.

Our big town event became the Fall Festival
of the Arts. Now the scientific and tech genius
of Leonardo is being expressed again.

Becoming Organized

I just bought an organizer with ten,
rainbow-colored bins to fill and label.
I have four others of the same design—,
slots for book print-outs, office supplies.
          I know where to find what I want.

My office the "The Grand Canyon"
with bookcases, file cabinets wall to wall.
The center has more storage places.
This central area was cleared to install track lights.
          I need to re-organize it all over again.

All these containers and contents were lugged
into the TV room to sort out, recycle, discard.
It is overwhelming to re-order and find niches
for what remains and replace in the center office.
          It seems overwhelming.

Thus the new bins on wheels to help
store some of the displaced items better.
I threw away old Christmas cards, decided
which books to donate or re-shelve.
          It is a quagmire of my despair.

I prefer to consider myself a collector not hoarder,
like my mini-museum of angels and small creatures.
But this stash is memories, reserves
and preserves I think I might need somehow.
          I must assemble my new organizer and start.

I am at the age I need to discard clothes, books,
papers, files, the detritus I just clutter my domain
with by default. To gather the energy and intent
to organize faster? My will is not there. I need energy
          to organize with others to persist and resist.

Re-Lighting

After over 50 years of hodge podge lighting,
we consulted with a professional
and we created an illuminating plan.

Lighting will be increased in my office, hall,
dining and living rooms. Later, heaven where family
and wordy-folk gather to play and critique.

First we selected the patterns and placement
of the lighting–some track lighting and solos
to brighten, blighted areas dimmed by darkness.

Then we selected the fixtures to enhance
the plan. Of course, I chose blue when
I could get away with it.

My office needed an upheaval in the center
where I had a huge storage area on a large
unused desk, now covered with boxes.

We need the installers to center the lighting,
so my husband hauled boxes and a bookcase
into the TV/guest room for me to sort.

We discover all kinds of books, photos, paper clips,
pens, envelopes–many items to donate or re-store.
A chance to ponder what to keep or let go?

Unfortunately, I am a collector–border line
hoarder-- who treasures texture and color
in every room and niche—everywhere.

When I die, my son threatens to bring
in a dumpster, so I'd better get sorting
to save what is useful and memorable.

Lumps of boxes filled with a wide
diversity of items to go through to decide
what will return to my office when re-lighted.

I will see more clearly the piles of memorabilia,
writing materials and collectibles once hidden
in the dark recesses of my workroom.

When my office is lighted more clearly,
I hope to illuminate my muse. My cluttered
home has just begun to be contemplated.

The Sidelined Chair

Along the side of the highway, facing traffic
is an upright, swivel, black office chair.
Who left it there and why?

Someone must have placed it upright
if it fell off a truck. Why did they leave it?
Did they expect someone would pick it up?

Is it an escaped corporate office chair,
of a fat-assed intolerable boss? Did
it just mysteriously bolt-or stolen

by a disgruntled employee, to let the owner
stand alone? Did a mover drop part of its
load and couldn't re-pack it? Drop unseen?

Perhaps a student left it and a homeless
person snapped it up from the curb to
push possessions and pets? Then discard it?

We have gleaners who recycle the leftovers
of the college crowd each spring. Is
this such an item from a dorm desk?

I have no idea how long the chair
has been there, as I do not usually drive
this route into town. It looks usable.

I hope it finds a home with someone
who needs a soft seat. It looks toward
the vehicles, pleading for drivers to stop.

But the traffic whizzes by and it is not
easy to pull over at this spot. Is no one
willing to adopt it? How long will it take?

Just part of the unwanted, left behind,
abandoned waste? Someone must have
used this chair. Why did they not take care of it?

Synchronization

You forgot that magic is real, and that synchronicities are the way the Universe gets our attention whenever it is trying to nudge us into new understanding or a new direction. Sara Wiseman

En route to exercise class I saw two
white-haired, bearded, old men riding
electric scooters. Is seeing two an omen?

The first was entering the main drag
from our side street and I swerved
to give him wide berth. Father Time?

The second drove across the intersection
on the crosswalk in a blazing red scooter
wearing floral shorts. Santa on vacation?

To see both within minutes, heading
in my direction was a strange coincidence.
My next mobility upgrade is a scooter?

I have walkers, wheelchair and transporter.
My husband hopes to be able to push
me so I do not need a scooter.

But seeing these two men riding
amid traffic with ease, made me pause
and wonder why I am seeing them.

I am used to seeing angel numbers
and feathers which I do perceive as omens.
Other synchronous events await interpretation.

Being aware, in the present, mindful
makes this chance more possible?
How do I interpret them?

On a trip, feeling anxious, I awoke
from restless sleep to see the motel room
lamp beside me flicker twice, then darkle.

Somehow I felt more relaxed, comforted,
that some energy was supporting me–
just like the geezers on the scooters.

Message in a Bottle

In this high-tech time with multi-sized screens
sending messages around the world faster,
why use slow bottles instead of machines?
Messages of connection or impending disaster?
        Bottles contain mystery, diverse needs.
        Convey love notes, doom notes. Message pleads.

Sending messages around the world faster
instead of bottled up, left to fate,
(which seems an archaic way indeed). Who's disaster?
But it's a method to send ashes, communicate.
        Expedition reports, crowdsourced studies,
        of ocean currents– some intent muddies.

Why use slow bottles instead of machines?
Some senders want to find stranger pen pals.
It may take years before someone gleans,
but it's the unknown, surprise that enthralls.
        Faster ways to express distress these days,
        but someone may not have access to these ways.

Messages of connection or impending disaster
bobble turbulently in waste-waves,
carry within it intentions of caster,
until a receiver picks up and braves
        opening dated contents and shares
        message to someone who cares.

Bottles contain mystery, diverse needs—
letters to actual or imagined love interest.
But it takes actual contact to plant the seeds
of how the relationship might grow, weather test.
        Bottled messages are meant to be found,
        but sometimes people are not around.

Convey love notes, doom notes. Message pleads
for connection to help or heal.
With bottled notes, our curiosity feeds
and we open up to what may not be ideal.
        Message bottles tossed into the sea
        get broken or if intact, picked up eventually.

Naming Names

Ten unnamed creeks
flow down the slopes of Marys Peak.
Now they have been named,
        ending a nameless streak.

Native American names selected
by 21 board members were accepted
by the Oregon Geographic Names Board.
        Approval is expected.

The names go to the federal level now
for formal approval. It could take a year, somehow,
there appears to be no opposition,
        to the results of this powwow.

When they began to undertake
naming they garnered support for those with a stake
in this decision: property owners, timber companies,
        governmental land managers could partake.

Local tribes provided names in
languages such as Kalapuya, Wusi'n, Yago'n
whose descendants still live in the area.
        Then the naming could begin.

Some names are Ahnhoots- Kalapuya word for "panther".
Pa'wint in Wusi'n means "cinnamon bear" is another—
Yago'n in honor of the Yago'n people.
        They worked together as sister and brother.

Indigenous people were here first. We know
this naming should have been done long ago.
Get more indigenous names on the landscape.
        A good start. More naming to follow?

Confused Muses

A miscommunication gap for this critique
meeting, confused these poetic women.
Somehow the date did not sift through easily.

For some it was misreading emails. For some
it was unsent emails. Others- it was lack of focus.
We had to rethink how we would communicate.

Someone would notify about the set monthly date
until January. We checked the list. All would
get an email and a reminder closer to the date.

At our age we cannot make a temporary change
of date for any reason without causing glitches.
It was so frustrating these gaps occurred.

We all are experiencing political burnout.
We watch news and write political
poems less. All are filled with stifled anger.

So when this snag happened, we wanted
to clarify intentions and devise a plan. Today
we brought mostly more light-hearted poems.

The darker poems were pondered seriously.
Suggestions for all the poems were helpful
and insightful. All are talented poets.

When they left, I felt more uplifted. Perhaps
we can correct misconceptions and find ways
to make the world less heavy word by word.

College Dreams

Last night I dreamed I was negotiating
with parents and educators to be able
to take my senior year at another college
and still graduate on time.

Fall 1958 I started my freshman year
at Central Connecticut State College–
later a university, a highly ranked
teacher's college at the time.

I commuted with my father who worked
in New Britain. I worked summers and
on campus as a guide. No student debt.
But it was not my dream college choice.

I wanted to go to top-ranked Columbia
University, but my parents thought New
York City was too dangerous and expensive.
So I didn't even apply for a scholarship.

I received several scholarships, but they
would still have been difficult to afford.
CCSC was accessible and affordable.
My father's mother lived beside the campus.

As I waited for my father, she offered
hot chocolate, Swedish and family history.
So I could have a living-on-campus experience,
we funded one term in a crowded two-bunk-bed room.

My boyfriend went to college in Troy, New York.
I took 21 credits the spring term before marrying him.
Then summer school and student teaching, I graduated
early with no senior year at the college.

Soon we were off to graduate school at the University
of Arizona–far from Columbia which I never even saw.
Was Columbia an illusion? What trajectory would
going there take me on? Sixty years later I do not know.

Over the years I experienced my credentials and
academic honors did not matter much. I did not teach
at the level I trained for. My dreams morphed and adapted.
Perhaps I did not risk or persist enough for my college dreams?

To Be Or Not To Be

Being is the path. Being is the way. You search for all for false distractions, you believe what isn't real, you travel on false paths, you push and push and push against time...when all you have to do is be. Sara Wiseman

Apparently being is not a question of
to be or not to be, but how to be
while you are being here?

Are we here to perform a mission?
To experience, to enjoy, relax, engage
or connect? Is all Now? How does that work?

Are we responsible for our actions?
Judged where or when by who?
A lone drone or clone? Cosmic spark?

What is being human in the multiversal
scheme of things? Even in this earthly
experiment? What's beyond just being?

For this time being, what should I be?
Am I just a matrix part of a program
with a quirky operator?

How much autonomy or freedom
of choice do I have? So many illusions
and delusions to sort through.

When I reflect on decisions I made,
how much control did I really have
and how was I influenced?

Being me this time, makes me wonder
where I should place my declining energy?
When I had it, did I make wise choices?

So much judging and challenges— many folks
with unequal, unjust playing fields. Whose design
was this? Perhaps we are a flawed conception?

Are we cosmic clowns, galactic pets, experiments
tweaked by DNA? A multidimensional, perhaps
simultaneous particle ort, fragmented eternally?

I am being a skeptical, noncommital agnostic
at this momentary stay in my being. My choice
or just part of the cosmic conundrum?

Night Senses

Rain gurgles and dribbles
        down the window
                behind the shade.

Motor murmurs mumble
        as vehicles rumble in the dark.
                Spacecraft or Earth craft?

Shadows of tree canopies
        flicker on the ceiling.
                Furniture is blurred, static.

I reach for the lamp-clicker for light, sit up
        and grab a book from the night stand.
                Reading might calm my restless soul.

What unseen and unheard essence could be
        surrounding me? Angels discussing
                my unique circumstances?

Are my dream scenarios not scripted yet?
        Characters not ready to perform their roles?
                My earth incarnation not willing to lighten?

What I can sense distracts me, I feel heavy,
        a sense of foreboding until reading
                guides me to quieted light and sleep.

Grief with No Name

No woman wants to bear/ whatever could be the name for this grief./ Even if she must bear the grief for all her days,/ it would be far too painful to be called by that name. Lucille Clifton

There is no name for mothers caught in the gyres of grief
after the loss of a child. No matter what one's beliefs,
there is no answer to the whys, the pain, grieving.

No matter the age or way the child died, the mother
is left behind, not called a mother to this child anymore,
not a widow, orphan or any other name for losses.

When our son died at nineteen in an accident far
from home, I went into shock, numbed, struggled
for months to resume commitments to the living.

In an Alabama court room, we learned injustice.
Our son's killer would not even get a traffic ticket.
In a parent grief group we learned ways to cope.

Grief brings misunderstanding of ways people
grieve, divorces and stress leading to cancer.
How do you answer: "How many children do you have?"

Birthed? Living? Dead? We adopted a daughter.
Did her mother grieve when she gave up two
of her six children? At least they lived somewhere.

I had no choice really but to try to carry on,
support the children I had. I wanted to make my son
proud of my choices and not withdraw from life.

People do not know what to say to you.
Do you want to hear how your child effected them?
What words and actions can comfort–even a little?

One told me my son died so I would become more
spiritual. I do not want anyone to die for me. A friend
was told- "Well, he would have gone off to college anyway."

I carried those heavy words for decades until an intuitive
connected with Kip who told me he was grateful I gave him
life to fulfill his mission. He had to go, but I was not finished.

He knew his death would hurt me. He would love and be
with me when I needed him. He freed and uplifted me.
Whatever names I am called, I will always be Kip's mother.

My Final Decade

In six months I will be eighty, my final decade.
Most likely, I should make a bucket list?
Mentally a list is being made.
Some changes I can't resist.
        Some conditions could stay the same.
        There are ones I am to blame.

Most likely, I should make a bucket list?
Should I fumble along without direction?
Should I confront things that make me pissed?
How do I make the best selection?
        Work on mind, body, spirit, service?
        What can I control? What will suffice?

Mentally a list is being made
of things to do and places to go.
What can I create? Who can I aid?
There is so much I'd like to know.
        What are my limitations
        to change to new situations?

Some changes I can't resist?
A new craft item, angels, family, friend.
Dance and art shows will persist.
I hope my poems will never end.
        Should I be writing down a plan?
        How long until I can?

Some conditions could stay the same,
my health issues could get better or worse.
My mind and spirit could dim their flame.
I can only do my best, of course.
        I wish I could find a pain remedy
        to cure any crone-related malady.

There are the ones I am to blame:
my lack of insight, imagination, caring.
Perhaps some wisdom came,
and I did not find it worth sharing?
        I'd like some joyful and fun celebrations
        in more of my contacts and occasions.

Waves of Thought

Listen to the sound of waves
within you.

Rumi

Unlimited Imagination

Never be limited by other people's limited imagination. Mae C. Jemison

Imagination is more important than knowledge.
If knowledge is limited, imagination does not have
to be as well. Imagination can transcend to new insights.

Any field progresses with imagination.
Freeing the mind to create is liberating.
If you judge too soon what flows, you block.

Everywhere I spot a manifestation
of imaginative power, I applaud
the magic, mystery, excitement it brings.

Theories come and go. Styles change.
Breakthroughs shift vision, expand awareness.
I revel in imaginative leaps which sustain me.

When the world seems dark and depressing,
I look toward innovations that bring light.
Engulfed in gloom, the fog hovers.

Dance is often in a spotlight. A beam
of radiance in motion. Art and science
can also shine, share enlightenment.

For me imagination is playing with light.
Letters on a page are dark until words
spill on white pages or screens.

I hope I'm not restrained and refrain
from exercising my free will. Light
is always welcome in my heart and mind.

The Writer's Job

Writers are not here to conform. We are here to challenge. We're not here to be comfortable–we're here–really, to shake things up. That's our job. Jeannette Winterson

Writers are not here to conform.
We are here to challenge reality's make up.
We're not here to be comfortable with the norm.
We're here really to shake up.
> Our job is to get people to ponder,
> to evoke emotion, action and wonder.

We are here to challenge reality's make up,
our place in the cosmos, role here on Earth,
to create new ideas to take up
to discover our mission for our birth.
> A writer and any creative endeavor
> can provoke expression to savor.

We're not here to be comfortable with the norm.
We must change to avoid extinction.
Our concepts must find a new form
or doom will be humanity's distinction.
> We must start to become "woke"
> or we might be the final folk.

We're here really to shake up
old ways of thinking for the new.
Hierarchies and injustices must break up.
We must connect to a better view.
> Writing jabs letter by letter
> pricks words to become better.

Our job is to get people to ponder
their mission and reason to be,
what conditions they are under
and find ways to become free.
> Can we adapt to the changing clime?
> Can we correct our path in time?

To evoke emotion, action and wonder
is many writer's quest and goal.
The Gaia connection can't be put asunder.
Can we reach and restore our soul?
> I struggle to remain an optimist.
> Meanwhile I'll persist and resist.

Processing Impressions

I don't think I could have happily stayed here in this world if I did not have a way of thinking about it, which is what writing is for me. It's control. Nobody tells me what to do. It's mine, it's free, and it's a way of thinking. It's pure knowledge. Toni Morrison

A trinity of sunflower blooms and dandelion bursts
amid the three handmade angels in the backyard.
Triple wind chimes tingling. One too lethargic to ping.

The unmown grass is raggedy and scraggly,
texturing the lawn, dotted with windfall apples.
No butterfly, few birds fly by. Wimpy wind.

The sky is overcast with scowling clouds.
The sun glimpses through casting brief,
faint shadows on the yard. I observe.

My heart breaks for recent mass shootings.
My body aches with crone conditions.
I await Aleeve to provide some relief.

I have just started reading Ken Carey's
Starseed Transmissions– but only the front
matter promoting the New Age viewpoint.

I tried to find him on the Internet with little
background information available. I like
to check out writer's intentions. We'll see.

Whereas I resonate with Toni Morrison,
mourn her passing, but she left her vision.
I like her attitude, her style, her imprint.

In writing I can explore what I learn and what
I do not know or understand, pose questions.
I do not judge how pure my knowledge is.

Are we all on a cosmic wave length, tuning
in to different frequencies, but part of a multiversal
consciousness? Is life an experiment or adventure?

Rain appears imminent. I pick up my blue pillow,
leave the metal chair uncovered to face the elements.
I'll ponder nature and reality inside.

Walking the Poetry Road

I don't understand my need to keep struggling with poetry–I just do it to please myself–hoping to sooner or later touch someone with my words–At times I feel I walk this poetry road alone. Roberta Plummer

Sorting through letters I found this note.
She expresses my feelings well.
My poetry I have been reluctant to promote.
My poetry's impact is hard to tell.
     We are all connected even when feel alone.
     I have long accepted I am poetry-prone.

She expresses my feelings well.
I began my poetry path when very young.
My word-play passion, hard to quell.
I love words flowing from hand or tongue.
     I write poetry most because I try
     to see words dance and then fly.

My poetry I have been slow to promote.
Over the years I've had many distractions—
teaching and family of special note,
as well as community interactions.
     But I keep walking the poetry road,
     sometimes carrying a heavy load.

My poetry impact is hard to tell.
Some feedback I can report
is encouraging. Some doggerel?
Kind readers have offered support.
     I want them to pay attention, question.
     Sometimes I offer a suggestion.

We are all connected even when feel alone.
Sometimes we are more open to receive,
other times we tend to postpone
listening to what others believe.
     Whether anyone encounters my poems,
     I go where my curiosity roams.

I have long accepted I am poetry prone.
Poetry brings me joy and release of thought.
I don't need a page or microphone.
My mind delights in what the cosmos brought
     for me to channel into form.
     Poetry keeps my heart warm.

My Muse's Vacation
The worst enemy to creativity is self-doubt. Sylvia Plath

For two days I have not written a poem.
The day before that I wrote four.
Is my muse on vacation? Left me?

If so, where would a muse go?
Visit another mind? Just kick back
in the cosmos, drifting mindlessly?

Maybe it goes to another dimension
and just gathers ideas to channel
into another creative mind?

Actually, it is my fault I did not write.
I had over-booked my days.
I did not take the time to sit and muse.

I did not go to the backyard and draw
chi and imbibe muse energy. Today,
I am eager to set aside time to write.

I have set aside a few hours this afternoon.
Now I am off to a massage after exercise class.
I hope the muse finds my body receptive.

I do not have an image of my muse to beckon.
It is some cosmic energy I connect with
that ignites my imagination.

I hope my muse returns from vacation or
a leave of absence revitalized, refreshed,
ready to set mind and fingers flying.

I apologize for any delays, missed appointments.
I treasure your presence. You bring meaning
to my life. Please never abandon me.

Nemeses to My Nisus

Nisus: an effort or striving toward a particular goal or attainment, impulse.
Dictionary.com

Each book I write is a particular goal—
a new nisus with each unfolding,
an expression of mind and soul,
ways of praising and scolding.
>Somehow I persevere despite distraction.
>The chance to word-play is the attraction.

A new nisus with each unfolding
as I ponder and wonder what will come.
What concepts am I molding?
Any creativity is welcome.
>I tend to let ideas flow
>and not edit as I go.

An expression of mind and soul
demands a lot of intention.
All my senses play a role
and seek my attention.
>I want to create to share
>and show others I care.

Ways of praising and scolding—
several sides and points of view.
What awareness am I embolding?
How can I widen my purview?
>There is so much I want changed,
>so many values I want rearranged.

Somehow I persevere despite distraction
of responsibilities, commitments, traumas.
Too much reality, escape to abstraction?
Too many conflicts, violence, dramas.
>Anxiety threatens to overwhelm me.
>How to breakthrough and see clearly?

The chance to word-play is the attraction
a time to dance the words into lines.
A chance to put discoveries into action
after finding ways to new guidelines.
>Writing is my passion and mission.
>I like to play freely without permission.

Pondering Poetry

Anyone can write a line of poetry. Try. That's my word: try.   Marie Ponsot

Marie Ponsot wrote ten minutes a day.
It was her commandment number one.
She believed with encouragement,
poetry could be written by everyone.

I love poetry in song or slam, on stage or page,
in oriental gardens, on walls, monuments or art.
Poetry has a diversity, intensity of expression
rhythm, sound, patterns–I want to be a part.

There is a place for most poets to find
an audience, literary or more accessible appeal.
Poets perform publicly or prefer more quiet lives,
search for meaning in the imaginary and the real.

How to define poetry? To me it's word-play,
controlling line lengths and forms
to mostly tersely tell a story.
Poetry loves to break the norms.

Ponsot was called a love poet, metaphysician,
formalist, translator, teacher who put aside her career
to raise seven children as a single mother,
but her dedication to poetry remained clear.

She admired English: Donne and Hopkins
while I seek poets of all genders and times.
Multicultural insights, progressive causes
capture my free verse and rhymes.

Ponsot just died at 98, which initiated this topic.
Her breadth is admirable, she believed
poetry needed only nurturing to flower.
She shared the word-seeds she received.

I'm not into judging, assessing a poet's rank.
I'm more into teaching methods to write
and to let the poet explore their own experience.
So many mysteries and insights to bring to light.

Most Memorable Poetry Readings

Robert Frost at Wesleyan
Folksy, sober Frost read in character,
then partied drunkenly with frat boys.
A biography revealed a nasty old man.

Elizabeth Bishop in Boston
Reclusive poet was giving a rare reading.
She was "ill-disposed", so we saw her documentary.
The audience whispered she was drunk.

Taylor Mali in Corvallis
Magnetic, energetic slam poet was magic.
I bought a pen with a scroll to unroll inside:
"On Girls Lending Pens." I see it everyday.

Maya Angelou in Corvallis
Vital poet, dancer and singer agilely performed
all three genres. She was indeed "Phenomenal
Woman". Every move and word enthralled.

John Berryman in Corvallis
In cigarette haze, slouched, grumpy, he did
not seem to want to be there. Monotone
bore. I did not want to be there either.

May Swenson and William Stafford YMCA in NYC
I'd seen Bill many times in Oregon. He was glad
to see an Oregonian there. I did not have the heart
to tell him I came to see my favorite poet, fascinating May.

Ursula LeGuin in Salem, Oregon
Calyx had published her poetry and prose. She gave
us a broadside as a fund-raiser. She stood for two hours
in her 80's as her adoring husband watched off stage.

Hive Mind

Collective consciousness. People aware of their commonality and think and act as a community, sharing their knowledge, thoughts and resources. Dictionary.com

Despite internet connections, global communication,
we have not achieved consensus for a hive mind.
We still have division and confrontation.
Clear global solutions are hard to find.
        Consciousness raising in each soul,
        for some it is the ultimate goal.

We have not consensus for a hive mind.
We do not have an unshakable belief
in something that can't be seen, bind
our Universal energy of Nowness, leave behind
        old constructs and hierarchies for new,
        rethink what we thought we knew.

We still have division and confrontation,
violence, misdirection, and confusion.
We discover different ends to contemplation,
can't sort reality from illusion.
        We are stuck in 3D duality's plight,
        the constant struggle of dark and light.

Clear global solutions are hard to find.
Inequities and injustice block our effort.
Lots to improve for humankind
in areas of sustainability, peace and comfort.
        Yet our fates are bound together.
        Climate crisis— a bellwether.

Consciousness in each soul
is a hope for a vibe-hike and New Earth,
to forge a cosmic connection and to enroll.
A deep inner knowing is needed for rebirth.
        We are born with true knowing.
        Inner awareness many are sowing.

For some it is the ultimate goal
to connect to God, Universe, One, Divine.
Clarity requires a lot of rigamarole.
For others life's mission is hard to define.
        The idea that we are ineffably much more
        is worthy for hearts and minds to explore.

The Wanderers

Not all those who wander are lost.   J.R.R. Tolkein

Some of us who wander off the trail get lost.
Some hikers found, others perish.
When we explore we bear the cost.
Sometimes we lose what we cherish.
> Some people are prone toward adventure.
> Others seek the known, to remain secure.

Some hikers found, others perish
while seeking the unknown, the new.
Some search for bucket list wish.
Some take off without a clue.
> Our destinations are in flux?
> Travel economy or deluxe?

When we explore we bear the cost
of getting there and of what we find.
Some speed while others exhaust
all their energy and state of mind.
> Do we ride the waves in the flow?
> What is our preferred way to go?

Sometimes we lose what we cherish
on the s/hero's journey, ring search.
Will we discover joy or anguish?
Arrive safely or in the lurch?
> Our fate remains unknown?
> How many beliefs dethrone?

Some people are prone toward adventure
others more in their head than in body.
Wherever they choose to venture
alone or with somebody,
> we like to feel in control.
> How much do we patrol?

Others seek the known to remain secure,
ward off fear, protect their possessions,
feel best with data and structure,
give in to their obsessions.
> I hope eventually
> Earthlings can be free.

When We Dream

When we dream, where do we go?
What dimension, what form?
We become an entity we don't know.
We don a new identity and uniform.
        Is my dream a multi-dimensional me?
        Do I play these roles eternally?

What dimension, what form?
Am I a hologram, light-being, or alien?
Some cluster of particles in a swarm?
From pasts or futures with cosmic kin?
        Some dreams are present alterations,
        with surprising tweaks to known locations.

We become an entity we do not know
at least in Gaia's 3-dimensional duality.
Are these alternatives, an unknown scenario?
Some unremembered life in some locality?
        Who directs the nightmares, brings the dark?
        Who guides the light dreams' illuminating spark?

We don a new identity and uniform
to suit the role we are playing.
To whose rules do we conform?
What audience are we swaying?
        Am I the only viewer?
        Others in dream also reviewer?

Is my dream a multi-dimensional me?
Soul-splices from the oversoul of All?
Will we ever know the mystery?
Ever grasp cosmic protocol?
        When our sleep-souls explore the multiverse,
        who decides what dimensions we traverse?

Do I play these roles eternally?
Do we dream to escape this earthly life?
Are we learning in dreams so eventually
we can move higher and lighter above strife?
        I ask my angels to protect my dreams
        so I don't fall victim to dark extremes.

When You Lie Awake at Night

Nothing like poetry when you lie awake at night. It keeps the old brain limber. It washes away the mud and sand that keeps blocking up the bends. Like waves to make the pebbles dance on my old floors and turn them into rubies and jacinths, or at any rate good intentions. Joyce Cary

When I lie awake at night, I greet a poem.
Perhaps a line drifted into a dream.
Perhaps I reach for a poetry tome.
Perhaps I glom onto a theme.
> In the dark, poems spring into light.
> In the dark, poems bring delight.

Perhaps a line drifted into a dream,
woke me up and urges I write it down.
More lines come. It would seem
a whole poem wants to tumble-down.
> Somehow I channel words from beyond.
> I am fishing in the cosmic pond?

Perhaps I reach for a poetry tome
piled beside my bed for my restless mind.
Can I lull myself back to sleep, roam
back to another dimension to find
> what is possible to know,
> where there might be places to go?

Perhaps I glom onto a theme
or begin a form to expand.
A trente-sei beginning is extreme,
but I have learned and understand
> when poetry wants to emerge,
> it will find a way to surge.

In the dark, poems spring into light
awake me with words I allow
to flow through me, enlight
my curious muse to follow.
> I welcome words night or day,
> any words that want to dance or play.

In the dark, poems bring delight
whether read, or wanting to be created
into poems I'm supposed to write.
Poems are always joyfully anticipated.
> When I lie awake I am never alone
> as long as I am poetry-prone.

Rumi's Ruminations

Be like the sun for grace and mercy. Be like the night to cover others' faults. Be like the running water for generosity. Be like death for rage and anger. Be like the earth for modesty. Appear as you are. Be as you appear. Rumi

Be like the sun for grace and mercy.
Yes, the sun can bring life and light.
But also sunburn, drought, urgency
to easy the climate crisis plight.
       The sun is an object of grace.
       The sun puts us in our place.

Be like the night to cover others faults.
Cover with darkness, or enlighten?
Faults can have impacts, concern vaults,
causing many to frighten.
       Can we offer to help with what mars?
       Or must we bear and heal the scars?

Be like the running water for generosity.
Some might prefer to lessen flow and dam.
Some assumed limpid responsibility.
Some clammed up, while others swam.
       Some just don't seem to care,
       while others hoard and do not share.

Be like death for rage and anger.
Both hard to smother, prefer to stuff or run.
Sometimes we are in threat of danger.
Sometimes we must confront what's done.
       What we conjure in our mind
       is not always erasable we find.

Be like the earth for modesty.
The Earth is bold, colorful, immodest.
What we do to Gaia is a travesty.
Sustain the Earth, to be robust.
       Let Earth breathe free,
       flamboyantly.

Appear as you are. Be as you appear.
Maybe we are not ready for a grand appearance?
Maybe what we appear should disappear?
Are we ready, prepared for our entrance?
       Sometimes we flunk the test,
       even when we do our best.

Seeking Blue Waves

Blue waves are not just in politics.
Blue water sought inland and in seas,
but plastic clogs our waters with
sluggish waves below polluted breeze.

Blue is my favorite color.
Red makes me see red— blood.
Blue in sky is preferable,
not a precursor of flood.

Everywhere fire, creatures bleeding.
Weather whirl-whips blue skies.
Glaciers calve, blue ice melts.
I feel blue, because we're unwise.

What is the color of waves in the future?
How much water and resources will be lost?
What banners will people wave?
Fire or ice? asked Robert Frost.

Why Not?

Feelings are much like waves, we can't stop them from coming, but we can choose which one to surf. Jonatan Martensson

So many possibilities to consider.
I have not committed many into belief.
I'm not into Facebook or Twitter.
I like news now with comic relief.
      Specialists in many fields bicker.
      What approach is slicker?

I have not committed many into belief.
Hierarchies, old cultural views,
appear in need of turning a new leaf.
I just don't share their purviews.
      We lack peace, justice–why not?
      We need sustainability. Not juggernaut.

I'm not into Facebook or twitter
but the Internet can be handy.
Fake news and disputes can be bitter.
Some folks are really underhandedly.
      What is true? What's current theory?
      Sorting the data makes me weary.

I like news now with comic relief.
Such dark misery needs some hope.
So much pain and so much grief.
It's hard to find ways to cope.
      Why not a design for humanity
      without all this insanity?

Specialists in many fields bicker.
Pompously stating what is true.
Meanwhile my optimism will flicker.
As I watch what they say and then do.
      The fate of the planet is on trial.
      Too many people are in denial.

What approach is slicker?
Will appeal to the exhausted populace.?
Who will be selected as the picker?
Is it out of the hands of the human race?
      Why not a loving, kind, supportive world?
      Why not let choice, freedom be unfurled?

Life Dancer

Life is the dancer and you are the dance. Eckhart Tolle

Life is the dancer and you are the dance
or is it life is the dance and I'm the dancer?
Either way, I like dance as part of living.

I'm more a mind-dancer these days.
I'm in the audience, not on stage.
I'm not the dancing star.

However dance manifests, I'm a fan.
Dance jiggles my molecules, perks
up my mood, engages movement.

Do I choreograph my own dance?
Do I have a terpsichore gene? A pattern
predetermined before birth?

The sway of nature, words spilling
on screen and page all have a rhythm
to dance to, to applaud.

When they talk about we are all connected
and synchronicities, could it be we are
all dancers part of an earthly routine?

We can dance as a troop or solo,
but by some means hopefully the urge
to dance gets us moving together.

What to Connect To?

"Those who have never known pain and adversity are as shallow as the waves lapping the shore." And what is wrong with being shallow?" I asked him." "What lies beneath shallow waters? Nothing. Its only when you go deeper that the ocean comes alive. The deeper you go, the more mysteries and surprises. Mara Rutherford

In spirituality a lifelong journey toward understanding?
In relationships long and short term resonance?
In planetary awareness how to be upstanding?
In our life's work will we get the best chance?
> In governance the disconnect is destructive.
> In what ways can we connect to be productive?

In relationships long and short term resonance?
Which ones end by choice or design?
How did they enter our lives, karma perchance?
When should we engage or resign?
> Which are lifelong and which are transitory?
> What will we learn? What remains exploratory?

In planetary awareness how to be upstanding?
Make the sustainable decisions, choose the good cause?
How can we confront denial and misunderstanding
and give hierarchies, injustices a pause?
> How can we help Gaia thrive?
> Will our youth have a future to live?

In our life's work will we get the chance
to fulfill our mission, be free to create?
Can we find the best circumstance
for our niche and to participate?
> How many connections enhance our work?
> Will we persevere to perk or will we shirk?

In governance the disconnect is destructive.
Division and ill-will, greed and poor leadership's flaws
lead to inequities, wars, become obstructive,
to progress or leveling playing fields, because
> they can't cooperate and trust,
> yet they could build a society that is just.

In what ways can we connect to be productive?
Is it up to each of us to be balanced and kind?
Lead with compassion, try to be instructive
for the highest intentions we can find?
> Can we connect, link up with our best instinct?
> Are we passively, pollutingly becoming extinct?

Soul Journeys

There are really only two stories: A Person Goes on a Journey or A Stranger Comes to Town. John Gardner

Sara Wiseman suggests if you are committed
to living from soul, you'll go on an unexpected journey.
Or you stay at home? Have you admitted
you are not ready for such a tourney?
        Walk your own path, let light lead?
        Walk in mystery? Profound indeed.

To living from soul, you'll go on an unexpected journey.
Or are you the stranger that comes to town?
Live a life that's twisty and churny?
Watch the world tumble-down?
        What prompts your soul's intention?
        What motives demand attention?

Or do you stay at home? Have you admitted
you might even have a soul to guide you?
What information is permitted? Transmitted?
What connects inside you?
        Make your own map, own guidebook?
        Give alternatives a look?

You are not ready for such a tourney?
Do you really have a choice, free will?
Is your destination cold, warm or burny?
Will your voice be for good or ill?
        More questions than answers perhaps?
        Make room for progress and relapse?

Walk your own path, let light lead,
follow soul's heart? Develop trust?
Your walk is unique. Plant your seed.
        What grows from your planting?
        What grace is the universe granting?

Walk in mystery? Profound indeed
to journey into the vast unknown.
Will your soul fulfill your need
to find direction, feel you've grown?
        Unexpected journeys on your way?
        How many roles will you play?

Ocean of Spirit

The wave is the same as the ocean, though it is not the whole ocean. So each wave of creation is a part of the eternal Ocean of Spirit. The Ocean can exist without the waves, but the waves cannot exist without the ocean. Parawnahansa Yogananda

Marianne Williamson suggests just like a sunbeam
can't separate itself from the sun, a wave
can't separate itself from the ocean. It would seem
we can't separate from each other, we have
      a part in the vast sea of love, divine mind.
      Our position is for us to find.

Can't separate itself from the sun, the wave
and all creation interconnected in All.
We must be curious and brave.
In such vastness, we are small.
      In whatever form we take,
      of this Spirit Ocean, we partake.

Can't separate from the ocean. It would seem
water is our source of being alive.
We can create our own dream
for how we want to thrive?
      All these particles, waves and orts.
      How is it each one probes and sorts?

We can't separate from each other, we have
to find a way to co-exist, cooperate.
Strength in diversity, we can chose to behave
peacefully, respectfully, appreciate
      the beauty and possibilities given us
      and stop creating such a ruckus.

A part in the vast sea of love, divine mind
sounds like a lovely incarnation.
What are the ties that bind
us to all of creation?
      I like creativity, imagination, kindness
      so we can leave discord far behind us.

Our position is for us to find
meaning and purpose for why we are here?
Enhance all beings not just humankind?
Rise above darkness and fear?
      I like the concept of Spirit Ocean.
      I'd like to wave it into motion.

Problems With Religion

People hate religion when the loudest proponents of religion are shown to be mercenaries for a leader who debases everything he touches. And yes, young people are leaving the pews in droves because too often the person facing them in those pews is a fraud. They hate religion because at a moment to stand up and be counted on the right side of history, religion is used as moral cover for despicable behavior. This is not new. Hitler got a pass from the Vatican until very late in the war.   Timothy Egan

Some people have a problem with religion
because believers do not act on the good intentions
of their beliefs. Too many predators and hypocrites.

White old men oppose abortion outside clinics,
and harass women who may not believe in their
faith to bend to their will. Shouldn't women choose?

Some clergy prey on their flock sexually
while proposing chastity and only
some accept same sex marriage.

Religion at its best follows the tenets
of compassion, caring for others, peace
loving charity and free choice.

Older white Christians support Trump's
toxicity because he is taking their side,
though he bullies, belittles, abuses others.

Christians, Muslims and Jews bomb
and shoot each other, fear replacement
by people who do not believe as they do.

"Do as I say and do as I do" does not
work with free thinkers. Reformations
and revolutions still hold women down.

Women rarely hold the positions of power.
They are oppressed in many cultures
by male-dominated beliefs.

Separation of church and state is porous.
Religion should not impinge on individual rights.
Politics should not overly control lives either.

Religious folks who do good work and do not try
to convert, can join all people of good will to hope
and help humanity to progress for the good of all.

Buddhism is Changing the Mind

Most important is to understand ourselves, then look for Dharma teachings that relate to our self-situation. Namnang Mingio Rinpoche

If we gradually learn Buddhist principles
we can put our minds toward the principles
we understand and align our thinking?

They call this alignment of thinking
and action "cultivation". We apply
this learning to change ourselves.

Only if we see our true current situation
will we find benefit from Dharma? I am
not much of a gardener and pretty old to dig.

But I can probe my mind to absorb concepts
if I try. Imaginings provoke reactions that lead
to actions that often make situations worse?

I always thought of imagination as a creative
positive force, but I can see we can delude
ourselves and perceive situations faultily.

If we can gain control and see things the right
way we can reduce suffering for ourselves
and others? Notice our imaginings and rethink?

We can cultivate this new approach over time
and reduce worsening emotional reactivity. Notice
problems, explore new ideas, improve ourselves?

Rinpoche encourages "You try and Dharma
nectar will fill your heart." Detach from good
or bad, liking or disliking, pain —for joy.

They urge don't "beautify" ourselves, pretending
we are better than we are. Is nectar drink for gods,
the raw material of honey or Dharma nectar for heart?

As a diabetic I need to watch the sweetness I ingest.
As a free-thinker I need to examine the concepts
I explore. Is imagination more important than knowledge?

Buddha-ish

Each of us must know our innermost hearts...Each of us must look into how we contribute in small and large ways, to the current crisis and turn in the direction of enacting the Nobel way—the way that leads all beings to liberation from all suffering. Abby Terris

Statues of Buddha show him as trim, sitting
cross-legged or fat Buddha standing. A seated
pudgy Buddha also is available.

When thin I could entangle my legs flexibly.
Now pot-bellied- -no way. Standing too long
hurts my arthritic knees. So I'm Buddha-ish.

I'm more Buddha-ish in thought. The more I read
about Buddhist practice, the more drawn I am
to its cooling our own fires first approach.

Some Buddhist suggestions: reflect on what we need
and our system of endless consumption, rethink
waste, words and actions that stir up others.

Act on behalf of the vulnerable and exploited,
focus on awareness of how our lives are woven
into the full fabric of life on the planet.

Our daily choices effect what comes next.
Realize our capacity as intelligent and aware
spiritual beings in an all-inclusive universe.

It is about personal responsibility for our own hearts.
Calm and clarify our nervous systems. Live ethically
independent of greed, aggression and confusion.

In an atmosphere of environmental changes
and political crises, ask questions about the system
of privilege, inequity, injustice, hate, denial.

I support these goals but do not take refuge in
Buddhist meditation. So I can only be Buddha-ish
in spirit- embody a womanly, feminist, activist stance.

Seesawing Through the Day

Not the waves, not the storms, but often ourselves sink our ships. Mehmet Murat Iklan

Thoughts and moods seesaw up and down
in response to the stimuli of the day.
Daily duality takes me for a ride.

How to sustain optimism as pessimism oppresses?
How to feel joy when fear and pain impinge?
Even keel possible? Balance?

How to revive drained energy?
Dark chocolate hourly?
Sip some caffeine?

Find activities to stimulate creativity?
Strive toward a goal? Immerse in work?
Meditate? Take a long vacation?

Each day I face dilemmas, choices,
challenges and blockages. Life's journey
can be exhausting, demands courage.

A seesaw is for play, requires, cooperation
to achieve highs and lows. As a crone must
I put away childish things? Seesaw always?

At the US-Mexican border an artist placed
three pink seesaws between the wall slats.
Children on both sides can play together.

The seesaws bring joy, excitement and togetherness—
a human connection regardless of borderlines drawn.
Children can see each other and play despite barriers.

The wall is a fulcrum. The actions on one side of the wall
impact the other side–a direct consequence.
Backward and forward. Up and down. Connect.

Uneasy

You never really know what's coming. A small wave, or maybe a big one. All you can really do is hope that when it comes, you can surf over it, instead of drown in its monstrosity. Alysha Speer

The backyard bears a bad case of apple acne.
Overcast skies glower over downcast sunflowers
before the rain showers begin.

A butterfly cowers in the garden dirt.
A spider web glistens diamond dew.
Puffballs spawn a dandelion rebellion.

The plucky dandelions give thumbs up
from the unmown lawn. Recent rain
revives their golden outbursts.

A brisk breeze spins the pinwheel,
swings the wind chimes. The cluster
of red-mini roses gently sway.

The anticipation of rain reoccurring
makes me watchful of the clouds, ready
to bolt with my blue pillow.

It is also chilly and my chi breathing hasty.
I want to absorb some energy and leave
for a massage to release my tightness.

Things seem ominous with occasional glimpses
of kindness and hope. At least no August smoke
drifting into the valley from hot spots yet.

Somehow I am unsettled, feel uneasy.
Sleep interruptions leave me weary and sore.
My protective stones must be still settling in.

My dreamscapes provided provocative scenarios
which upon waking remain illusive and unattainable.
How many dimensions am I operating in?

I return to daydreaming and coping with conditions
which appear unbalanced, in need of enlightening.
Where to turn next? What to confront first?

Stuck with Distraction

The soul is not here to check off to-do lists. The soul is here to expand and to understand, and to participate. Sara Wiseman

Apparently you can't get to Now from a to-do list.
We must be still in order to discover
the full extent of our addiction to distraction.

Getting still can bring tremendous emotion
and unease when we take away all the sensory
and emotional load of distraction.

Apparently stillness helps us know our truth.
We are to look at, sit with and feel
what we really feel. I feel overwhelmed.

Apparently if we have a very busy life
we have strayed from our soul path?
Can we expand by doing nothing?

We arrive in Now when we are brave enough
to see what lies beyond distraction.
Trump is a master at distraction. He wounds.

I really don't want to focus on distraction
and Now is not a pleasant reality. I don't
want to drop out, but shout for change.

Apparently my soul is not expanding as it should
because I find in distraction the trigger for change.
On TV I select channels for my needs and mood.

I want to activate, participate, understand all I can.
I may not have a to-do list to achieve this, but
I do not want to be still as Now clamors toward disaster.

Regrets

All of our regrets come from a lack of courage. Bronnie Ware

Bronnie Ware listed the top five regrets of the dying:
1. I wish I had the courage to live a life true to myself, not the life others expected of me.
2. I wish I hadn't worked so hard.
3. I wish I had the courage to express my feelings.
4. I wish I had stayed in touch with my friends
5. I wish that I had let myself be happier.

I wonder what I will regret before I die
and what I could do to realize them beforehand.
Do I lack the courage to face regret? Dying?

Should I look at my life from the perspective
of my death or what I can manifest in the future?
Am I too busy puzzling out life to do so?

I spend a lot of time trying to figure out why I was sent
into this incarnation and what is my life's mission?
Love, light and service? How?

I did indeed come in interesting, but turbulent times.
I find myself concerned about the sustainablility
of the planet and what I can do for descendants.

I am old, but I align with the youth marching
for their future against predatory adults
and those in denial of their impact.

Will I regret I did not have the courage and insight
to do more, will my top five regrets be focused
on myself or the survival of others?

I continue to ask the big questions and dwell
on my connection to All—my part in the cosmic plan.
If multidimensional with an eternal soul,

my earthly regrets may be just part of a complex
scheme I will remain unknowing about? Will
I regret not knowing? Will I retain the courage to try?

Cultural Waves

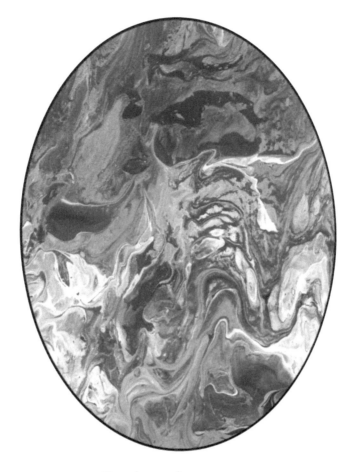

Society is a wave.
The wave moves onward,
but the water of which it is composed
does not.

Ralph Waldo Emerson

Human Prehistory

Found in Greece, the fossil hints that humans left Africa thousands of years earlier. Carl Zimmer

Homo Sapiens is the latest upstart?
Other hominids played a part?
Will we find another human oopart?

As technology gets better,
new discoveries unfetter
concepts not following the letter.

We bred with others like Neanderthals.
Many hominid branches met their downfall.
What was the origin of them all?

There are gaps in the record.
Evolution not a responsive cord?
What prompted the homo horde?

Did modern homo sapiens all evolve
and in waves began to move
out of Africa, create a new groove?

Dates of departure keep getting pushed back.
Current origins are under attack.
Something's out of whack?

They follow DNA, bones and tools,
learn Neanderthals were not fools.
They followed different species' rules.

Modern humans have round heads.
Neanderthal's skull longer instead.
They were faster, stronger, interbred.

Anthropologists dig their ditches,
hoping to find more homo niches,
providing new prehistory riches?

I am sure many ancient peoples were lost,
victims to a homo holocaust?
How many attempts? At what cost?

I do not know what scientists can retrieve.
What data can we receive?
What theories should we believe?

Virtual Influencers

When the Taliban destroyed an ancient
statue of Buddha in Afghanistan,
a 3-D light projection restored the image.

Lil Miquela is a computer-generated influencer
made of pixels to look like a 19 year old.
She has a bevy of beautiful friends.

She has 1.6 million followers online
and she doesn't exist–like Buddha statue.
She was created from scratch to sell.

Bella Hadid and her digital counterpart
Miquela Sousa are in a Calvin Klein
commercial which caused a stir.

A virtual news anchor, fake models
and a digital Colonel Sanders
join fleshy, real influencers.

Human simulations have dealt cards
in Las Vegas, made music with Gorilla
band. Lived in the Sims video game.

Fable Studios is "the virtual beings company".
Lucy can read and respond to viewer's
reactions. There are digital teachers.

The company makes digital creations.
You can build a two-way emotional
relationship with some creations.

Virtual beings could supplant digital
home assistants and computer operating
systems like Amazon and Google.

Many characters are stereotypes with
impossible body-image standards.
Back to Barbies?

Virtual influencers are not regulated.
Companies should insure product claims
are not misleading and substantiated.

In an environment of deepfakes,
bots and frauds what is truth in
advertising? Can you trust messages?

These avatars work non-stop, maintain
perfect image, don't need retakes.
Avatars are the future of storytelling?

Nanoinfluencers, kidinfluencers
and petinfluencers–fake beings
everywhere influencing us.

Manipulated video makes Nancy
Pelosi appear drunk and spoofs
Colonel Sanders. Mona Lisa speaks.

Brud is a "transmedia studio that creates
digital character driven story worlds".
Like a 3D animated Disney creation?

Bermuda, a Trump supporter accused
Lil Miquela of running from the truth.
Lil Miquela is a robot. Is Bermuda human?

As AI advances and hybrids prepare
for space explorations–will our species
become a virtual creation and no longer "real"?

Virtual influencers are becoming more
common, but fans engage less with them.
An avatar is a mannequin in a shop window?

Genuine influencers offer peer to peer
recommendations. Who programs avatars?
I tend to ignore social media and influencers.

Dutch Scouting: Dropping

*You just drop your kids into the world. Of course, you make sure they don't die,
but other than that, they have to find their own way.* Pia De Jong

A Dutch scouting tradition called "dropping"
drops off groups of children in a forest and
they are expected to find their way back to base.

The mostly pre-teens are dropped miles away
from where they are camping, with only a primitive
GPS as darkness falls and they are alone.

The GPS points in the right direction, but
sometimes adults hide in the underbrush
and make noises. Some adults trail them.

But adults do not lead. This is to make
them resilient, face adversity. The children
are in charge to find their way to base.

Dutch children are taught to not to depend
too much on adults. Adults are to let children
solve their own problems. Children are in charge

as they trudge tired, disoriented and hungry
through the forest. Many children live this life
without a forest in rural and urban locales.

How many American helicopter parents
would send their children into a forest
infested with predators, clowns, wild animals?

Children already confront poverty, bullying,
drug abuse, depression, suicides, accidents,
why add a forest? Pushing boundaries is fun?

Dutch participants wear high-visibility vests,
guidelines mainly geared to traffic safety.
Climate change may limit campfires.

Some Smartphone smugglers could use
an app for any troubles and directions.
Children live in hazardous places, fewer forests.

In hard times children are encouraged to keep
walking, to keep going. Children are often blindfolded
to the drop-off to throw off their sense of direction.

Hours later when they reach base, their mind
and feet are tired. Adults feed them, let them sleep.

Driving

Emissions per rider in a full bus or train are vastly lower than a car...
Americans drive millions of miles every year, helping make transportation the
biggest contributor to United States greenhouse gas emissions. Tony Dutzik

Here we have been blaming planes and cows
for their emissions being a problem. Add cars.
Consumers and scientists add their know-hows,
try to reduce Gaia's wounds and scars.
>So much pollution in our atmosphere.
>How are we to breathe here?

For their emissions being a problem–add cars.
1,089 million metric tons of carbon dioxide,
one-fifth of county's total emission output mars
efforts to reduce the climate crisis divide.
>A ten percent cut is about the same
>as taking 28 coal-fired plants out of the game.

Consumers and scientists add their know-hows.
They can car-pool or work at home more.
A cut of 1,350 miles per year shows,
a not easy but realistic way to lower our score.
>Reduce one-third of trips less than two miles.
>Walk, take public transit, bike to increase smiles.

Try to reduce Gaia's wounds and scars.
Find ways to travel without cars, bus, bike-share?
Focus more on Earth's viability— not Mars.
Help make other people become more aware.
>Gas is cheap, public transportation poor,
>make people want to use cars more.

So much pollution in our atmosphere.
Drive less, fly less, eat less meat.
Lack of actions make us fear.
Help alternative solutions to compete.
>Each us must do our part.
>Deniers, please have a change of heart.

How are we to breathe here?
Are we expecting divine or alien interventions?
Who do we expect to interfere?
Who will aright our intentions?
>We need policy changes,
>more information exchanges.

Flight-Shame

The climate movement shouldn't only focus on air travel. A more effective way to reduce carbon emissions would be to pressure political leaders into taking decisions that have nationwide and global effect. Anders Leverman

Some travelers are part of a growing movement
to shun air travel because it produces high
levels of greenhouse emissions.

Fighting climate change will require bold actions
by leaders and citizens around the world
if we are to reduce impacts of our pollution and waste.

Greta Thunberg, youthful activist no longer flies
but uses trains to get to her environmental
marches, meetings and speeches.

Airlines say flying accounts for 2% of man-made
pollution, yet reduce costs which leads to soaring
airline emissions: 710 million tons in 2013.

This year's CO_2 will reach 926 million tons:
a huge chunk of the annual carbon budget
of 2000 kilograms per person to be sustainable.

Wildfires from heat waves also rage as youth fear
the future. Flight-shaming comes from many sources.
We need to stop adding carbon to the atmosphere.

In Oregon Republican legislators boycotted
going to work to block a vote on cap and trade.
Governor Kate Brown hopes to override them.

I resolved after a recent flight I would not fly again.
I will take a train or drive. We must inform and
guilt-trip individuals to minimize their carbon footprint.

The air will become more un-breathable. The ground
and oceans more plasticized. Habitats mined
and damaged until Earth is uninhabitable

Flight Shame is a small sacrifice to make, with many
more needed if humans are to survive. Can we act
in time to avert extinction of all life?

Lights for Liberty

The main thing is that you're showing up, that you're here and that you're finding ever more capacity to love this world, because it will not be healed without that. Joanna Macy

Over 700 cities held protests over conditions
for immigrants to this nation. In neighboring town
over 120 people gathered at the court house.

Lights for Liberty partnered with local communities
–20 around the state of Oregon—
as Trump announced new I.C E. arrests.

Lights of Liberty is "a coalition of people...dedicated
to human rights...and all human beings have
the rights to life, liberty and dignity."

In Albany they gave speeches without a mic.,
cupping hands to be heard. Tee-shirts
and signs said:

No human is illegal on stolen land
Cage Trump, not kids.
Close the camps.

People are standing up to make the world better,
to deal with climate change, women's rights,
inequities, prejudices, waste, pollution...

If we love the world and want to prevent
extinction, we must confront issues
that challenge, take positive action.

Protest, petition, vote. All the flux and flow.
More love, less hate. More listening less talk.
Most of all act and connect. In time?

Send Him Back

After another sexist, racist attack on "The Squad",
his Trump rally chanted "Send her back". They
are all born American citizens, only one naturalized.

If only we could send him back—to jail or to
disempower his bullying, distraction agenda
as he wreaks havoc with the environment and world.

Many of us are weary of his old hierarchical ways,
his predatory behavior, his stupid comments and
tweets, filled with errors and misspellings.

He cages children, mistreats immigrants, poisons
minds by refusing to ban pesticides, he wants
to mine our National Parks, pollute the air and water.

The world sees him take us out of treaties. He
is a inflated balloon in diapers, national disgrace.
Trump followers do not care what he does.

All the Trumpets want is their money. Economy
over morality and decency. His cronies are crooks.
He must be impeached or removed from office.

How long must we suffer? We must repair his damage.
We have to address climate change which he denies.
Can we act in time to save the planet? Send him back—Hell?

Writing the Wrongs to Rights Huddle

Tomorrow night after a summer hiatus
our writer women's Huddle is ready
to march, persist and resist again.

We have been forwarding all the emails
with pleas to support various good causes,
contribute to politicians who promote change.

We will be face to face again, spout
our frustrations, bring pamphlets
for planned events we can attend.

We will make signs for urgent acts
to effect the climate crisis, carry them
with striking students leaving classes.

Greta Thunberg will be with them after
meeting Obama and addressing Congress.
Soon to provoke the United Nations into action.

Women of all ages and places must
fight for the future of children. Why give
birth to dismal death and suffering?

Our Huddle protests for our grandchildren
who may not live to bear children.
We may become extinct by then.

What kind of a world do we want to leave
for our progeny? We're nasty old crones
wanting to kick ass and get things done.

Angel Wings

I feel toward the flesh hanging from my arms that I now have angel's wings and then I laugh at myself because crones aren't always angels. Sometimes we transform into bitches, refueling our wrath, and when that happens, I whisper, "can you see me now?" Mary Susan Selby

My angel wings are more solid–like meat on hooks.
We are not just sweet old ladies or bitches.
We are stronger than it looks.
We can be good or bad witches.
      We can be strong and howl.
      We are not ready to toss in the towel.

We are not just sweet old ladies or bitches
relegated to the stage wings.
We are aware of our glitches.
But we are still discovering things.
      A lifetime of looking outward and within.
      A life of times abundant and thin.

We are stronger than it looks
with our wrinkling bodies, but sturdy souls.
We pondered many male-centic books
and still created our own she-roic roles.
      #MeToo and #Timesup, long time brewing.
      Our anger at injustice is still stewing.

We can be good or bad witches
in a real world, not fairy tale,
create whatever our wand twitches,
in a universe where angels prevail.
      Perhaps it is obvious
      angels are autonomous.

We can be strong and howl,
still protest people's negative impact.
I want to add my indignant yowl
to try to keep the planet intact.
      My body may ache, I may groan,
      but I want to connect, not stand alone.

We are not ready to toss in the towel.
It may be a fabric with little thread.
But we must not hide in a cowl,
but face life with courage, deepen our tread.
      We can't shrink into the sidelines.
      Wing it. Even as flight pattern declines.

Song of Herself

Her happiness floated like the waves of ocean along the coast of her life. She
found lyrics in his arms, but never sung her song. Santosh Kalwar

So many women never get to sing their song
lacking opportunity or confidence,
they never discover where they belong.
Their existence lacks concrete evidence.
     Shadowed by men, serving others' need,
     often they are victims of abuse and greed.

Lacking opportunity or confidence
told they were not made of the right stuff.
They were not to exert their intelligence,
made to feel they were not enough.
     Cultural roles limited chances
     and the dreams equality enhances.

They never discover where they belong,
talents never brought to fruition.
All dreams they hope for and long
for die, part of their sad attrition.
     Who wants to be put on a pedestal?
     Women want to be treated as equal.

Their existence lacks concrete evidence,
accomplishments erased or not recorded at all.
Their treatment defies sane sentience.
Why follow flawed, erroneous protocol?
     So it is not surprising,
     we see feminism rising.

Shadowed by men, serving other's need.
Abused into silence, they are speaking out.
Listen and act with good intention, they plead.
It's women's time to shine, without a doubt.
     Men have made a mess of things.
     Women need to toss their rings.

Often they are victims of abuse and greed.
Women free yourselves to sing your song,
do your own thing, unbind, indeed
call out and show them where they are wrong.
     Sing and share the women's word.
     Time women were freed and heard.

Leveling the Playing Field

We got pink hair and purple hair. We have tattoos and dreadlocks. We got white girls and black girls. And everything in between. Straight girls and gay girls... This is my charge to everyone, we have to be better. We have to love more. We got to listen more and talk more. It's our responsibility to make the world a better place. We have to collaborate. It takes everybody. This is my charge to everybody. Do what you can. Do what you have to do. Step outside yourself. Be more, be better, be bigger than you've ever been before.

Megan Rapinoe

It is not just on the sports fields,
but on all fields of endeavor.
Equal efforts, equal yields.
Equal opportunities, equal favors.
    Justice demands we correct mistakes.
    Equality means upping the stakes.

But on all fields of endeavor,
ways are found to discriminate
so a select few can savor
and determine who can participate.
    Diverse voices are speaking loudly,
    demanding a place and acting proudly.

Equal efforts, equal yields
do not get equal compensation,
power falls back on cultural shields,
leaving the left out in consternation.
    Racism, sexism, "ism"s divide,
    victims to what others decide.

Equal opportunities, equal favors
available to all, treated fairly—
no special waivers,
face the challenges squarely.
    We can do better. Love more.
    Be bigger than before.

Justice demands we correct mistakes.
We need everyone to cooperate.
We must exert all it takes
to bring changes in attitudes and climate.
    Not just weather, but in all relations
    requires connections of all nations.

Equality means upping the stakes
to release contributions from everyone,
to see everyone partakes,
old limiting ways are undone.
    Take responsibility to do our part,
    best we can with mind and heart.

Between the Fence Slats

Our backyard adjoins three neighbors.
Each neighbor put up a fence: four fences
of wood and wire, four diverse designs.

The fences have slats. Three styles of vertical
fence are unpainted. The wire attached to wood
by beige posts makes small silver rectangles.

Cats pass through as well as small wild critters.
We can see slices of neighbor's property. Birds
and squirrels perch on them. Walk the beam.

Part of the US/Mexico border wall has steel slats.
Three pink seesaws bridge the gaps. Children
from both sides can play, bobbing up and down.

They are observed by Border Patrol agents
and Mexican soldiers. Prototypes and etchings
of the "Teeter-Totter" Wall have been in museums.

Artists and architects have designs for a "Burrito Wall"
by inserting a food cart. A "Wildlife Wall" would
allow endangered species to pass through freely.

The seesaws display creativity and showcases
the fact people of both sides of the border get along
despite the wall. At some places both sides

party in the river under the watchful eyes of guards.
Our backyard fences attempt to delineate property
lines which other creatures ignore. No gates for people.

If we want to visit, we talk through the fence or
we go to the front door. Do I want to keep the fences
blending with nature as much as possible?

What could I poke between the fence slats to enhance
connection? A handshake? Fruit? Part of me wants
to paint the slats in vibrant colors–a rainbow mural?

Woodstock 50

Woodstock remains controversial—
a contrast to the Vietnam War which
killed 109 during the festival time.

Another big divide of values and beliefs.
Young people were drafted or protesting
what was going on and killing them.

Two died at Woodstock amid 400,000.
One of heroin overdose, one run-over.
But mostly a peaceful, musical event.

They had a Please Force, not Police security.
The poorly organized event had shortages of water,
food, toilets, and medical care amid a downpour.

But volunteers brought in supplies, flew
in military doctors, Hog Farm fed and cared
for them. Attendees shared whatever they had.

Yes, they had drug problems, we do now.
If held today, we would face an opioid crisis,
white supremacy, mass shooters amid wars.

They did not have cell phones and held candles.
Perhaps cell phones would be held for light.
Today perhaps better planning for such a crowd.

They have scheduled a better organized event
in the area, less freedom and more security.
They plan to control the number in the audience.

But today we face similar problems as then.
We are sharply divided over many issues.
Youth today are marching for a future.

Many remember Woodstock as a spiritual time,
where cooperation, community, generosity reigned.
A brief glimpse, despite hardships, of hope.

Music brings people together world-wide.
Climate crisis is global. Woodstock has a vision:
we are all in this together to create a better world.

Climate Justice March and Rally

Part of Global Climate Strike September 27th, 2019
Riverfront Commemorative Park, Corvallis, Oregon

Hundreds of town and gown climate activists
gathered at various locations to march to the park.
OSU and high school students and staff, Interfaith
and community members carried signs, chanted,
drummed through the streets to the Riverfront Park.

An estimated 500 people came, about the same
as last week's march as part of a week of events
centered on the climate organized by the Corvallis
Climate Action Alliance which is composed of several
local climate action groups. Rally to start 3:45.

Since we were juggling two wheelchairs, we decided
to park adjacent to the park and greet the marchers
for the rally. My husband, Court and I watched
them set up booths and stage, practice tunes.
It was sunny, but with menacing clouds and wind.

A stage sign encapsulated it all: **Strike** because
the Earth is heating so fast. **Strike** for a Green
New Deal. **Strike** because Exxon knew way back
when. **Strike** because those who caused the least
suffer the most. **Strike** because solar power is so
cheap now. **Strike** because it's a sweet planet.
Strike because...

Another stage sign: Carbon offsets our bridge
to a greener future. Seed for the sol.org.
Climate action Now. All hands on desk.
Local solutions with action bring hope.
Create a better future. We rise for a green future.
We can build a fossil fuel free world.

Soon we heard drums. Folk singers stopped singing.
A forest of signs streamed onto the lawn. Interfaith
members from Beit Am, Quakers, many denominations
waved banners and signs. Then OSU and high school
students chanted into place as well as community members.

Signs. Government rollback to get rid of wrong I.C.E.
Listen to the science. Youth for Climate Justice.
Systems Change. We need a green new deal.
Keep the oil in the ground. Let the youth be heard.
I displayed : Fossil Fools: Respect Gaia. Time's up.
Go green near OSU Scientists for a Better Planet.

Chanting and sign waving until rally starts.
Songs while marchers gathered like "Celebrate the Water."
Several speakers like Susan Salafsky the publicity chair
urged people to vote with your ballot, attention and dollars.
A Shawnee OSU student spoke for indigenous people
and reminded us we were on Champinefu land.

Molly Monroe of the Sustainability Coalition builds
backyard habitats and raised butterflies. She lead
children to the Willamette River to release 100
butterflies to migrate to California where
they are depleted.

We had an Interfaith prayer suggesting we take
in the blessing and step up for all beings's viable
future. High school student Molly Gottfried
said we were not to be silent or passive. Corvallis
High has solar panels and composting. 15 year
old Bianca Curtin conducted a family survey on
their habits which needed to become more climate friendly.
We must listen, learn and keep trying.

Storm clouds overcast sun. Wind whips cold winds.
Another student Carson Lommers mentioned we
are at a turning point. But other countries have acted.
It is not fair the youth must do this, but their repsonsibility.
All must work together and act.

Julie Williams on the staff of Corvallis High started
the Green Club. She mentioned the blessings
and burdens of young people. It is a time for change.
All we need is love. Action for love of planet. Invest
in the future, not in coal, oil, gas. Plant trees. Save
soul of the world. Everyone has something they can do.
Build on what you can. All is necessary. No excuses.

A father worries about his children. 50% of fossil fuels
used in last 27 years. The impacts are beyond imagining.
We should end fossil fuel subsidies and move away
from extraction and consumption to conservation
and renewal. Humanity is awry. Life itself is at stake.

OSU scientist Bill Ripple urged all to unite with science
and listen to Greta Thunberg's UN speech.
All hands on deck. Then there was a delightful
play by a local playwright, The Masque for Gaia.
It was very funny on serious climate issues.
It made fun of fossil fuels, greedy CEOs. Outlandish
costumes of Gaia, weather, coal, oil, gas and death.
Theater in the Round performed it.

Court took Dick Weinman and wheelchair home
after his performance in the play. I stayed for
the remainder of the rally. An OSU indigenous
longhouse woman named Louie Whitebear,
talked about indigenous actions and how we
were guests on Kalapuya land. We are to live
in balance and let Earth purify herself.

Jill McAllister, a Unitarian pastor offered
a prayer for this "holy moment". We are blessed
to be in this moment now. We are called to do this
and are not to be distracted by anger. We work
out of love not fear. Be courageous and strong.
Start again every moment.

A song. "What is not Here" Then Charlyn Ellis
a Ward 5 City Councilor spoke about city
projects. A petition of climate demands will
be brought to city officials after the rally. It is part
of a movement around the country to make
climate crisis demands for assessments
and accountability. There is a climate action plan.

Finally the Raging Grannies– one over 90 lead
the crowd in the song "Sing for the Climate".
The audience was given lyrics in sheets in a large font.
"We need to wake up... We're on a planet that has
a problem... Make it greener. Make it cleaner.
No point in waiting; or hesitating. We must get wise,
take no more lies and do it now." The refrain for
each verse. "We need to build a better future.
And we need to start right now."

The crowd dispersed carrying their signs, chatted,
herded children. As I waited for Court to return for me
I talked with a friend. We were part of a global
climate-centric event. The scowling skies urged
all hands on deck if we were to see Gaia shine.

Healing Waves

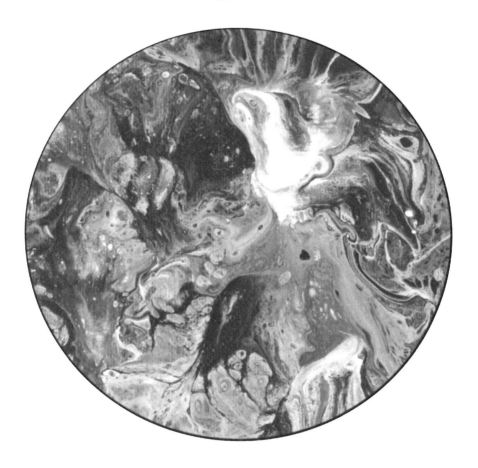

The cure for anything
is salt water,
sweat, tears,
or the sun.

Isak Dineson

Second Attention

The first attention is held by the mind and in its highest form is expressed as Love.
The second attention is held by the whole body and its highest expression may be
called mystery, compassion, ecstasy or even perhaps Fun. Will Bradley

The second attention is indescribable.
Shamans learn to clear practicalities, return
the magic to mundane and imaginable.
Beyond the visions of this world they turn.
      We can dream into second attention,
      if that is our intention?

Shaman learn to clear practicalities, return
to second attention to accumulate
the essence of our experiences, to learn.
Both attentions coexist. Only first can relate
      its highly descriptive detail, written or in speech?
      We can learn what second attention can teach?

The magic to mundane and imaginable–
unnameable, unspeakable into words?
To distinguish between sacred and mundane attainable?
Or ineffable as wind-lifts, ripples of birds?
      The first attention is upheld in ways we interact.
      The second is private world, connection to divine act.

Beyond visions of this world they turn
to focus on both attentions in harmony in a person.
If balanced and when society churns
to embrace personal connection to divinity in unison
      then no basis for religious conflict?
      Less oppressions to inflict?

We can dream into second attention?
Exercise our innate ability to develop?
Can we follow techniques for retention?
A new way for humanity to cope?
      First attention obsessions unfulfilled alone?
      Second attention is bold dreaming prone?

If that is our intention
to probe this attention mystery,
to understand intellectually or in confused convention,
it's fun to imagine mystically.
      Distinguish between sacred and mundane?
      Create a world we can sustain?

Visit with a Shaman

My shaman friend selected 18 stones to protect
me from dark energies, heal and uplift my energies.
A match spread smoke on them to consecrate them,

after he washed them all, dried them, blew three
breaths of air and meditated on them. He had five bags:
three blue and two translucent red with golden stars.

Then he placed them in my bedroom, around
my bed in a triangle. One blue bag above my head
on a doorknob. A large black one in a cradle

made to lift my head for my bed. I must wash,
dry and breathe three breathes to cleanse
this big one of negative energy occasionally.

Crystal, amethyst, labrycite, obsidian, jasper
and a few others exude energy for me
to be in better condition to bring light.

He has helped me before. Recent years
have really drained my reserves. I especially
love the blue and purple stones.

Surrounded by these special stones at night
and during naps, I hope to cleanse and refresh,
abolish dark energies from my being.

Heavy Homework

After a session with a shaman
to help me deal with toxic folk,
for my heavy homework I can
write down resentments, evoke
      what needs cleansing and clearing,
      what negativity am I hearing.

To help me deal with toxic folk
I'll confront what is hard to face.
Was it some cosmic joke
we dwell in this same place?
      Why do I feel this energy drain
      which leads to frustration and pain?

For my heavy homework I can
delve into what concerns me.
Can I find solutions, rework. ban
what causes this distress...eventually?
      Are they in my life by mutual choice?
      Will I express discoveries, add my voice?

Write down resentments, evoke
my higher vibrations and insights.
Why do I allow them to provoke
stress, to engage me in their plights?
      Can I learn to step back, observe
      and find the best way to serve?

What needs cleansing and clearing?
What am I willing to let go?
What remains that is endearing?
Just what should I know?
      I need my soul to reveal
      what I need to do to heal.

What negativity am I hearing
that commands my response, attention?
What steps should I be cheering?
How can I reset my intention?
      As I write down what I resent,
      I hope it is time well-spent.

Escapees

As I head to the overcast backyard
to gather chi and balance chakras,
I drape a pink neck warmer around my neck.

I hope to heal and distract myself
from the discomfort and ache
radiating from my neck and shoulders.

A dried stalk at my feet escaped the mower
at the edge of the patio, sways
in the breeze beside clipped green grass.

A brief tune drifts from the distance
with a wind-chime response. Birds
rustle and squawk, take flight.

The green hose squiggles across the lawn,
pokes nozzle in ripening strawberry patch,
near roses and sunflowers released from seed.

The heavy angel weathervane does not shift poses.
Tiny windfall apples fall from branches.
Blueberries, plums and pears are ready for picking.

White clover prevail around the mound
left by the chopped cherry tree. A few
yellow clover dwell in a depression.

As the sun escapes the clouds, restores
shadows, I linger to absorb its rays—
my neck warmer — an upside down horseshoe?

It is an unlucky horseshoe? I guess it
depends on the perspective. I take it off
and go inside for a heating pad.

The Blue Feather

Beside the green hose, point into earth,
a blue feather waves in the wind.
I walked over to check it out.

I picked up what appears to be a Stellar jay's
feather–mostly blue with an edge of gray.
To me a good omen. I am delighted.

The gray, overcast sky seemed to get
patches of blue. The wind chimes
danced in the brisk, cooling breeze.

Last night I had a dark nightmare.
I could not make a sound for help.
I was afraid to go back to sleep.

My massage therapist found black cords
and threads in my chakras, which she
removed and replaced with golden light.

She suggested I get crystals in and beside
my bed to protect me. I called a shaman
friend who said he would find some for me.

A book I ordered will not arrive until next
week, so my shields against dark energies
can't help me until after the weekend.

When I saw the blue feather, my spirits
soared, I balanced my chakras and chi
with renewed energy and hope.

This blue feather is the fifth in my found feather
collection. Another grayer feather leans against
this blue beauty. Three smaller feathers surround.

They are beside my computer, hopefully sending
positive vibes to tide me over in dark times.
Finding feathers uplifts my soul.

Fear of Falling

Ever since a virus toppled me
to the floor, cleaned me out,
ended me in the hospital
in quarantine–I have feared falling.

They said with my arthritic knees
I should have a walker to prevent
falling. So my journey with walkers
began inside and outside the house.

For a few years I have been fall-free,
then last night–boom. We parked
the car in the garage, I pried myself out
the door and tripped on a rug.

I careened into boxes, smacked concrete.
My left knee was impacted most. I could
not get up. My husband could not lift me.
I could not get on my painful knees.

He dialed 911 and three firemen put a blanket
under my arms, one pulled and two pushed
me to my feet and into a transporter chair.
For several hours I iced my knees inside.

It is time for the next step–a life alert system.
My body is just not reliable. I can't expect
24 hour surveillance from others. This aging
gig is a pain in so many ways.

This morning my left knee is tender but I am
ambulatory. Soon I will lay down and ice.
We were going to two art fairs today, but I think
we'll just go to one. I am lucky I'm not more hurt.

My husband has feared my falling as well.
He knew he could not lift me alone. The TV
ad of a woman who has fallen and can't get up,
is now me. I fear it might happen again.

Healing the World

Each of us has a unique part to play in the healing of the world. Marianne Williamson

New Age thinking suggests not only are we all connected
on this planet, but also to the universe. We are each
soul-slivers of energy and consciousness of the cosmos.

Many believe they are messengers of light with a mission.
The trick is to figure out our calling and to bring light
to the darkness, not just for humanity, but all life.

We each could find something we could contribute
to steward this imperiled planet? Upgrade our
intentions and actions? Cooperate and nourish?

Youth are marching to protect their future
by increasing awareness and urging prompt
action on climate change and gun control.

Violence in wars, mass shootings, abuse,
increased suicides and mental illness,
plastics and pollution encroach and kill.

Some predict the extinction of clouds,
increased glacial melt and dryness,
causing migrations toward the poles.

Leaders with misguided intentions promote racial
divides, identities splintered in gay and straight marches—
policies, divisive not cooperative or accepting diversity.

People are planting trees, changing habits
to be more sustainable and help those in need.
These feel good stories keep hope alive.

We might try making icebergs in submarines,
but it would take millions of them. Produce less
methane by curbing cows and power plant emissions?

Fossil fuels replaced by alternative sources
of energy? Drive less? Live more sustainably?
Inequities and injustice prevent solutions.

Many of us are exhausted by the challenges
we have so little control over. Many feel no matter
what we each do, it will not be enough or in time.

To heal mind, body, spirit, planet for a cosmos
we do not fully understand, can be overwhelming.
Human consciousness is resilient and hopeful enough?

I ink out my pain and curiosity, leak thoughts
to the page which few will read. I search for ways
to heal myself, others and to become a cosmic citizen.

My part may not be enough or in time, but I have
to try to do my bit in the swirl of particles manifesting
patterns beyond my control or comprehension.

Cosmic Waves

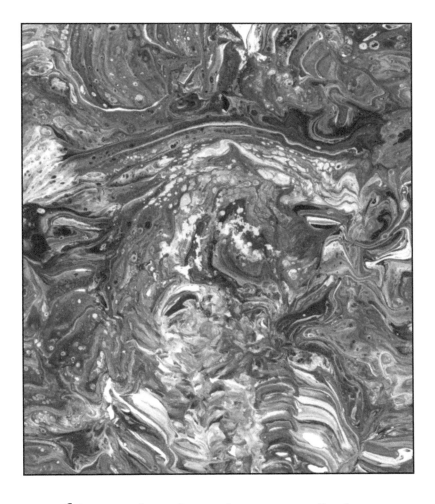

Physics has found no straight lines.
Instead, the physical universe consists
of only waves undulating back and forth
allowing for corrections and balance.

R. Buckminster Fuller

Why Does the Universe Exist?

Not just this universe but multiverses await
answers as to who, what, when, why, how.
People throughout time remain flummoxed.

Scientists, philosophers, theologians,
curious folk in many fields of endeavor
have no definitive answers to any part.

I listen to the theories, bemused,
knowing I will remain unknowing.
I've acquired a tolerance for ambiguity.

For some questions I am unlikely to ever
find answers, so I just have to cope and
try to act kindly and sustainably.

What is existence? In what forms and places?
Is this all a cosmic joke or serious experiment
in how to create diverse worlds and realities?

Why is humanity so inept and ill-equipped
to steward Gaia and all its inhabitants?
Why conduct an experiment with such deficient handlers?

The purpose of each universe may be different.
Was it really created from nothing? My cause
and effect mind can't conceive of nothing.

How can I create new ways of being
to reduce destruction and suffering
when perhaps change requires chaos?

We cling to comfort and yearn for safety,
adopt beliefs that provide some relief. I cannot
judge others' choices when I fumble my own.

Multidimensionality and eternal souls provide
challenges toward infinity. Do we ever get a
break from being? Have nothing to do?

The Multiversal Omnisparkler

Who is the cosmic coordinator of ALL?
Is the head honcho divine? A flawed god
who has representatives in each universe?

Is the cosmic matrix a web, wave or a pyramid?
Is there a chain of command, some organizing
purpose for consciousness at all?

Is the cosmic concept still in committee?
Is there is a multiversal omnisparkler
in charge of operations everywhere?

How is the energy distributed?
What is the source of All composed of?
Embodied or not? Embodies or not?

By the time the experiment reaches Earth,
has the essence been erased, muted?
Is a bemused archangel governing Earth?

If we are all sparks connected to all others,
how do we know? An uneducated guess?
Our hierarchies based on false assumptions?

Are Earthlings just sparks meant to flash
and flame on this planet until we are burned out?
Our challenge is to sort light from dark intentions?

When we leave sentience here, do we take our
soul-spark with us for a new dimensional experience
in a new form? Recycling, renewable energy?

In cosmic consciousness, what are the compositions
and missions of our cosmic companions?
Do we get different menus? How much choice of items?

Religions and science take different approaches
to unknowing. Whatever method of seeking
answers and coping, the basic conundrum is elusive.

For me the Multiversal Omnisparkler and Sparklers
might vote for bringing light into the infinite darkness.
I remain open to interpretations, but unaligned.

Cosmic Connections

> *Somewhere on some other planet orbiting some very distant star, maybe in another*
> *galaxy, there could well be entities that are at least as intelligent as we are. Suppose*
> *they have very different sensory apparatus–they have seven tentacles and they have*
> *14 funny-looking little compound eyes and a brain shaped like a pretzel.*
> *Nevertheless we can be confident that these creatures would discover the same*
> *fundamental laws. Some people believe otherwise and I think that is utter baloney.*

> Dr. Murray Gell-Mann who peered at particles and saw the universe.

Origin stories of global ancient cultures feature
sky or star beings coming to Earth in noisy vehicles
spewing fire and smoke, then land to impart knowledge.

They tweaked DNA and created civilizations.
Are we starseeds from a cosmic life-seeding
program which our space explorations might join?

Humans created religions and beliefs that worship
supernatural, higher beings— our progenitors,
that supposedly guide our lives even today.

Others claim we came by panspermia, water
inside comets and meteorites with the formula
to begin life forms on Earth. Cosmic breeding?

Directed panspermia is cosmic seeding from
inside metal capsules which contain water
and life elixir, targeted here by advanced beings?

Water seems to be an essential element which
we share with other planets. In our vast oceans
in many unexplored regions are myriad forms of life.

Some people have witnessed spacecraft
emerging from the ocean from an undersea base.
Cosmic-carriers deliver the life spark to land and sea?

The octopus has 50,000 to human's 25,000 genes
and is intelligent. Adaptable in form and coloration some
predict we could become the planet of the octopus.

If we flub up and destroy breathable air and pollute
land and sea, perhaps the octopus or aliens will land
and clean up damaged habitats? Strange things happen.

Could hybrid or robot beings recycle and replenish
the Earth or with more durable bodies take the space
race into a new humanoid or new beings' home?

Alien abductees say they have seen alien hybrids
from their eggs and sperm. Some may be living
among us, undetectable. Mission unknown.

Waves of starseeds from various planets may be
incarnating to raise our vibration for an uplift to the Fifth
Dimension? These light-bringers could prevent extinction?

Are we holograms? Imported cosmic creations?
An experiment to see the best life-fit for this planet?
What starseeds could replace us? Life starts here?

We are not alone in the multiverse. All of creation
just for some flawed, fleshy forms? We may never
know how life originated here. Maybe our time's up?

The multiverse could send replacements to restore Gaia.
Wherever they come from, in whatever form, hopefully
life will prevail to enliven and enlighten existence.

Bridging

According to some gurus we are bridging
from the 3rd to 5th dimension, spending
time in the 4th dimension bridge.

We are on a roller-coaster up and down
between dimensions, our energy signature
seeks sovereignty and resonance.

Many espouse we are an energetic
vibration or frequency and we must purge
density and choose clearly for higher self.

In doing this cleansing we are clearing
the collective and the Earth as well,
be an eye of the storm with love.

We are to be an energetic bad ass
as we purge and choose to resonate
on a higher frequency.

We are to clear out from the inside
and choose wisely from what's
outside until we make the shift.

Sometimes as we stand on the bridge
we might want to jump off as the work
is hard. But the lure of getting across is high.

Experiencing heaviness, darkness
and density is not easy, but necessary
if we and others and planet are to uplift.

Apparently our energy field extends
one and a half feet beyond our body.
What do we want and what to cast off?

We need to choose how to respond
and uplift as we clear inside, engage
outside of us, align, resonate.

We are to explore what to purge.
Don't wallow–get rid of the dirt. Increase
your vibration., expand frequency higher.

We must love and honor resonance
as we get unstuck from the bridge.
Apparently it's like learning to ride.

3D is like a trike, three wheels.
4D is training wheels on two wheels.
5D is riding a two-wheel bike.

We help the child learn through it.
Love them whatever stage. My
mother could not balance a bike.

Yet, I would say she resonated
with love well. We are here
to shift consciousness,

not just for ourselves but collectively
and whole planet as light-bringers.
We serve All. Big job.

So we are to become aware,
awake, raise our vibe, become
a five vibe tribe. Maybe someday?

Tweaking Our Vibrations

Much has been written, spoken and channeled about the Fifth Dimension and humanity's ascension into this new realm of existence....many "ordinary" people are now having their own experience, visions and inner "downloads" about the Fifth Dimension. Vidya Frazier

Apparently my life task is to raise
my vibration so the planet and all
its beings can shift to the Fifth Dimension.

Apparently dimensions are not places
or locations, but levels of consciousness
that vibrate at a certain rate.

Apparently the higher the number
the higher the vibration. Most people
are 3D or 4D itching to be 5D.

Apparently we need to resonate
with a higher vibration to shift to that level
of consciousness. Try to avoid pull backs.

Apparently we incarnated on Earth
with 3D operating systems which
are very limited and restricted.

Apparently 3D has rigid beliefs, many
inflexible rules, duality, judgment,
and fear, is subject to gravity and density.

Apparently some people are on the 4D
bridge where moments of spiritual awakening
and heart opening are experienced.

Apparently we'll feel clearer and lighter.
There is a sense of upliftment, more
spaciousness, less rigidity. Quiet.

Apparently we just need to ask for help
from higher dimensional beings to make
the transition to a higher vibration.

Apparently we can take our bodies with us
into the fifth dimension. This shift is supposedly
the next step in humanity's evolution.

Apparently we need to take care of our bodies
as transformation is hard on the body, brings
pain, aches, exhaustion and flu-like symptoms.

Apparently there is no right way to do this.
We can let go of old patterns, release negative
energies, judgments and thoughts. Not easy.

Apparently if we can keep our vibe higher
we can move through the 4D bridge faster.
Clear your intention to let go what does not serve.

Apparently many believe this is not a fairy tale
though 5D sounds like one with peace and harmony,
oneness with all life, respect, love, compassion.

Apparently we get equality, justice, respect,
no poverty, hunger, crime. Abundance for all.
No fear. Trust in the Divine. Utopia?

Apparently we will be divine inter-dimensional
beings as we were meant to be. Such an ideal
world has not revealed a time-line. We're in process.

Apparently 5D is a whole new level of reality
in which our consciousness is love, peace,
compassion and spiritual wisdom.

Apparently this plan has existed for eons,
We are perhaps at the mid-point in 2012
and it will unfold, picking up speed.

Apparently in this world of struggle and
suffering, we imagine or dream of another
reality and yearn to go to such a Home.

Apparently all souls have a choice to go
to 5D if they have assimilated sufficient light
to hold the energy level. Many will stay in 3D.

Apparently those who stay to shift with Earth
will go through some intense and rapid changes
as mind and body shift into higher consciousness.

Apparently we are in "transitional" or "the end times".
One reality structure is collapsing and another emerging.
Whatever does not serve us in the shift must fall away.

Apparently old relationships, careers, life approaches
out-dated sense of identity and negativity hold
us back in a lower vibration.

Apparently my heavy, dysfunctional body wants
to let go and lighten, my mind and spirit want
to enlighten. I am ready to let go of a lot of detritus.

Apparently I am not ready to depart and sort
through my clutter and my collections which
bring me such joy. I may be held in 3D longer.

Apparently I should sit outside in the sun more,
especially in cloudy Oregon to absorb all the light
I can. Polish my inner light? Keep dark chocolate?

Apparently when I am ready to cross the 4D
bridge (and I am eager to do so) I can experience
my dreams, fantasies and highest intention?

Apparently I need to remember I am shifting
not just for myself, but all lives and Gaia.
Let's hope extinction does not come first.

On Being Psychic

When we connect with the Universe in this way–through our psychic understanding–what we are really doing is living from our soul, instead of from our mind. Our mind is based on separation, on being "right", on being linear. Whereas our soul is whole. It is based on Oneness, on allowing. Sara Wiseman

During my journey through this incarnation
I have met several intuitive individuals.
They have my respect and appreciation.
They understand cosmic protocols.
    They heal, they counsel, they foresee.
    They can intuit what we might be.

I have met several intuitive individuals
whose life's mission is to raise understanding.
Some have their personal rituals,
to enhance the powers they're commanding.
    They see beyond the physical, the hidden.
    They see causes which to some are forbidden.

They have my respect and appreciation.
My life has more clarity when I listen.
They assist me to bring in my creation.
They shine my soul, make it glisten.
    Much good and joy in my life has come
    from their sharing. They're so welcome.

They understand cosmic protocols,
connect me to my beloved departed.
Puzzle through earthly folderols
and get my imagination started.
    Just because I can't do as they do,
    does not mean their gift is not true.

They heal. They counsel. They foresee
what I have not figured out.
They open limitations to possibility.
They bring more certainty than doubt.
    They believe we are all connected,
    They are companions I've selected.

They can intuit what we might be.
They provide a broader insight.
They have guided and comforted me.
They have set my spirits aright.
    These special abilities are so needed.
    I am glad they were cosmically seeded.

Eternally Ensouled?

From some perspectives, we are cosmic beings
going in and out of matter in many locations
in the multiverse, connected in some plan.

Currently my soul-spark is embedded
in a fleshy, bony body on the planet Earth,
experiencing what this quirky reality has to offer.

Our dreams conjure other realities and I have
no idea how many lives I have lived or where.
Speculations are this is an eternal process.

Living as a light being has its perks to me.
Weightlessly cruising the cosmos, perhaps
encountering other soul-specks I knew?

This incarnation supposedly is for soul growth
and this Earth experiment sure has its challenges.
Since time is a linear construct, how much time

do we have in this context to get things working?
Billions of human beings are crashing the planet
for the chance for redemption or to provoke extinction?

If we have simultaneous lives, in multiple dimensions,
things get complicated quickly. Our equipment can
sense only this world with inklings toward other realms.

Beliefs in angels, guides, aliens and otherworldly
beings could help these wandering souls cope
with the realities they are dealt— momentarily.

If this batch of human bodies is to ascend
to the 5D or higher consciousness, perhaps
we are making a cosmic leap in soul progress?

So much is unknowable. I try to explore diversely
and ponder theories on what is going on. When it is
time for me to make a transition, I expect a surprise.

Limitations

There are no limitations, unless you create them yourselves. Anything is possible. You are only limited by your own imagination. Dolores Cannon

My imagination is limited in 3D reality's darkness.
I can imagine a 5D Golden Age of light,
but my imagination does not make it happen.

My mind is glutted with climate crisis, violence,
injustice, inequality. My imagination alone
can't make sustainable change. I'm crushed.

My body aches and its mobility compromised.
I can imagine how it once was, but the limitations
of age and culture leave many dreams unfulfilled.

My imagination is not healing me and preparing
me to face challenges. I can't control outcomes.
Imagination is often illusion.

My mind sees two mass shootings, inaction
by leaders, people's best interests not being met.
I feel overwhelmed, helpless, hopeless, limited.

My body feels weighted down. Its chemicals
out of balance. Maybe by depression?
Can imagination relieve any of Earth's trauma?

Gurus tout a shift is coming. The cosmos wants
Earth to thrive? A DNA tweak might help and
a vision of a caring, supportive populace prevail?

My imagination needs an upgrade. My mind—
light-enhancement. My body— some pain relief.
I no longer believe anything is possible.

Thunder Moon
　　July 16, 2019

The Thunder Moon is a half-blood partial eclipse.
A full lunar eclipse is a blood moon.
　　　　In North America we can't see it.

Africa, Australia, South America can.
Parts of Europe and Asia can see part of it.
　　　　In North America we can't see it.

Also called a Ripe Corn or Buck Moon, it's named
for frequent July thunderstorms. No matter
　　　　in North America we can't see it.

Apparently intense light waves stream
from the cosmos. We should get some, but
　　　　in North America we can't see it.

Perhaps it is a metaphor for what North America
just doesn't see, but other continents do, because
　　　　in North America we can't see it.

Before the Super Black New Moon

Before the Super Black New Moon
tomorrow, I go to the backyard to ground
before blasts of comic energy empower me?

I am to align with divine energy to open to my truth,
highest self, newness, expanded opportunities.
Sirius rays could enhance my DNA? Worth a try.

So I haul my chi chair to the middle of the lawn,
pull up my purple hoodie to protect my face,
let the sun bake my back and aches.

I am pale as a ghost and ghosts don't tan.
I risk skin cancers. My thoughts flit like
the butterfly, who finally finds a companion.

Beside me in a beige, blotch of dry grass
amid some pesky, frisky green whiskers,
I spot a tiny white feather, thumbnail size.

Two fingers pick it up. Some detritus
flicks off. I wonder what bird this is from?
Birds tick and click in the canopy unseen.

I have moved away from the solid shade
of the roof-line, near the light-spotted shadows
of the trees, to let light lift, warmth heal me.

Still one peach left. One sunflower on
seven possible hosts. This stalk about six feet
inches above angel Tootsie weathervane.

Maybe a young angel in training
shed my mini-feather while fledging.
I almost lose my grip as a daydream.

Thumb and finger hold the feather tight
as I go inside to place it in my feather jar.
Someone placed a small green tennis ball

on prone angel Bottom's belly. I put the orb
on the blue table beside him. Perhaps angels
have come to play today? I'd like to think so.

On Black Moon Supermoon Afternoon
    Dumbledore: a bumblebee

On this auspicious day as the mercury retrograde
ends and a supermoon blasts transforming
cosmic energy, I go to the backyard to imbibe chi.

Such a clear, blue sky with crisp, shadows.
Brisk gusts usher in wind- budged breezes,
nudge apples from their boughs.

Dumbledores and butterflies buzz by.
The lone sunflower a beacon for landing.
Birds of different breeds call quietly.

In such a refreshing scene it is easy
to get swept away in anticipation
for the uplifting, soul-cleansing rays.

It is hard in such a warm, sustaining place
to envision the climate changes to come,
whatever energy the cosmos might send.

I huff breaths of fire, try to balance my chakras
without proof of success. Concentrate on
absorbing warmth and releasing stress.

I am reluctant to go inside, cool off,
leave the tinkling wind chimes. I carry
the silent phone, not sure what calls me.

I am open to the possibility the Supermoon
could connect us to All. Perhaps the cosmos
is trying to help humanity clean up our act?

Men on the Moon

Twelve men left garbage on the moon's surface.
Humans wasted the "man in the moon".
What? Too macho to clean up after themselves?

If they bring anything to the moon, they should
take back their debris, not just deface
the surface, collect and take dust and rocks.

Americans made six trips to the moon.
This female symbol had no women.
Maybe they would not be so messy?

Even the ladder label was sexist:
Here men from the planet Earth first set foot upon
the moon, July 1969 A.D. We came in peace for all mankind.

We came for all mankind? What if there
are moon dwellers? We came for them too?
What did we leave? Garbage.

Neil Armstrong tossed a "jettison bag" filled with
empty food pouches, bodily waste, scraps cluttering
their cramped spacecraft. Recycle on earth.

We should not send anyone into space if we
are not willing to make room for our trash
and not trash the other planet or moon.

Five littered landing sites. Messy men
with greed to exploit resources, to learn
about space whether welcome or not.

Can't we unintrusively observe? The moon
hosts American flags, footprints, plutonium
in generators, a Bible, "transfer Assembly"

which are bags of urine. Other bodily waste scatters
around the moon except some kept for testing,
$2 bills cache, Falcon Feather from gravity test.

A ceramic art tile the size of a thumbprint, designed
by five artists supposedly was hidden on Apollo 12,
might be there. An ethnocentric dump remains.

Cosmic Chaos

Strange objects from galaxies far away,
black holes forming, perhaps some planets
host life, but some seem to think they should
be composed of the same stuff, bio-beings.

Today scientists announced the multiverse
might be younger and then they guessed
older, until finally admitting they do not know.
Supernovas explode, meteors strike.

Our planet is not the most tranquil either
as we face a climate change challenge.
We faced extinctions before, but this time
we are a really big part of the problem.

With the only constant being change,
it is hard to get a firm grasp on things.
Tonight is a harvest full moon exuding
strong vitalizing energy–some say.

I am not sure what is going on, why or
how the multiverse was planned–or not,
what was the start? From nothing seems
kind of an excuse for we don't know.

Well, now whatever is expanding
and at some time the sun will suck us up?
By then people may be long extinct
and some other consciousness might

be wondering, just like us, what is going on
and why are we experiencing such chaos?
Does not seem much we can do, but gaze
at the beautiful, powerful moon while we can.

What's Out There?

A million people responded
on line to a hoax to Storm Area 51.
Are there aliens inside?

Several sources speculate
aliens are there. Others want
to know. About 100 came.

But 2000 came from all over
the world to alien-themed events
in Las Vegas and Rachel.

The US Navy revealed video
of UFO craft which humans
can't identify or build.

Crop circles leave symbols
created by unseen energy
to download into our minds.

These encoded symbols are in
a light language, blocks of information
our subconscious will decode someday.

People report being abducted.
Scientists have no proof, but think
we must not be alone in the universe.

As the curious gather at Alienstock
in Nevada, at A'le-Inn in Rachel, millions
of others were striking for Earth's climate.

On same day someone twittered
the choice people made about
what the future may hold for humanity.

"There are two types of people in this world,
those who storm area 51 and those
who strike for the climate."

Perhaps aliens will save us from ourselves
and help protect the future for our progeny?
Whatever comes, I hope we work together.

Storm Area 51

The Internet created the Storm Area 51 event
as a joke, but millions responded and plan
to invade the secret US Air Force base in Nevada.

It is heavily guarded. County Commissioners
denied a Peacestock 51 event there, so
who knows how many will show up?

Due to occur Sept. 20-22, the curious
participants want to know if they have aliens
and reverse tech alien spacecraft on site.

The secrecy has provoked many rumors
and many alien theorists stoke the flames.
But the area is ill-prepared for the onslaught.

It is a desert so little food, fuel, sanitary facilities.
Traffic jams, makeshift campsites, no
medical facilities. Like Woodstock without rain.

Two events are approved for Hiko and Rachel–
tiny desert towns. Rachel has an alien tourist
shop. It is near Las Vegas.

Cell phone service could crash from
the increased volume of calls. How many
emergencies could not get help?

We took our grandkids to the boundaries
of Area 51. You are warned not to trespass
and can see the surveillance. Spooky.

We saw a bus carrying workers going home.
Windows shrouded. Much security involved.
How will they pass to get to their jobs in a mob?

Many alien conspiracy theories exist. Many
believe governments know about aliens here,
but do not believe the public is ready to know.

This might not be the best way to find out.
Causing a state of emergency and perhaps
violent confrontation could make matters worse?

SpaceX Rocket Launches Satellites

The 24 separate satellites–including an Air Force satellite for basic research as well as the cremated remains of 152 people–were packed together in an independent payload that will be gradually deployed to a variety of orbits.   Shannon Stirone

We hurl more and more detritus into the sky.
Tomorrow smoky fireworks for fourth of July.
A Tesla and now cremains could crash and fall.

This is the third trip for Falcon Heavy.
Before it carried telecommunications equipment.
Musk says this launch was the most difficult ever.

SpaceX has landed and reused its rockets again.
But what about all the space junk orbiting
for a traffic jam and collisions?

An attempt to land on a drone ship called
Of Course I Love showed the vehicle's mission
landed explosively into the sea.

Some of this launch's cargo includes Carl Sagan
inspired Lightsail-2 cubesat carrying a solar sail
the size of a loaf of bread. Light-Sail 2 has mylar sails.

Over 20 miles of them will open to collect as much
sunlight as possible. Photons have momentum not mass.
The cubesat has a momentum wheel steered from ground.

It hopes to go 450 miles above Earth using sunlight
to enter high orbit for a year. Solar sailing can provide
an alternative fuel for spacecraft, reach deep space.

The Green Propellant Infusion Mission, a NASA payload
is testing a most environmental friendly fuel. Most spacecraft
use toxic hydrazine. Hazmat suits needed for humans nearby.

They are trying AF-M3ISE which has never been used
in space. It is a green propellant which is less of a threat
to humans and also more efficient.

A Deep Space Atomic Clock.will track missions to deep
space. Now agencies use slow radio signals. Robotic
probes call home to confirm current time and location.

Space agencies need a more timely way to track
their spacecraft and future human missions.
Will time run out for us down below?

Atomic clocks track vibrations inside an atom
like cesium to measure time accurately. Aboard
Global Positioning Satellites atomic clocks

help to precisely triangulate distances traveled over
periods of time. But the technology has never been
used in deep space. Future missions navigate like GPS?

All these creative spacey minds focus on cosmos while
earthbound problems compound and we send debris
to space. We could get so cluttered we can't see stars.

All these missions for naught if we can't sustain Earth.
Our cosmic legacy is littering satellites and cremains
in the cosmos above a devastated Earth?

A New Dragonfly

The mission to Titan is in part to study whether the moon, is or was, home to
life. The idea to use a drone comes after years of studying alternatives, like a hot-
air balloon or even a boat. David W. Brown

Dragonfly is a drone-style quadrocopter to explore Titan,
the largest moon of Saturn, craft scheduled to launch in 2026.
Meanwhile on Earth climate change flying might face a ban.
Scientists and politicians can't agree on a climate fix.
        Why go to Titan to explore?
        Are funds for environment needed here more?

The largest moon of Saturn, craft scheduled to launch in 2026,
contains standing liquid water on its surface.
It also has an atmosphere and methane. Life mix?
Camera's on Dragonfly view's underground and moon's face.
        A battery charged with radioactive power
        works two and one-half years to empower.

Meanwhile on Earth climate change flying might face a ban.
Pollution building with each flight threatens air.
Some people are not flying, take train when they can.
People are waking up to dangers and becoming aware.
        Can we act in time on Earth to make a correction?
        Why not focus here? Why Titan better selection?

Scientists and politicians can't agree on a climate fix,
yet sponsor a "Shark Tank" for deep space exploration.
Punch and Tracers missions will go to sun, they transfix
curiosity. In 2024 mission Artemis goes to our moon, our nation
        and globe ignores the climate change threats.
        Youth march and protest, live with regrets.

Why go to Titan to explore?
Complex organic molecules might fall from atmosphere?
Sunlight drives moon's photochemistry and more
energy to prime life there? New Frontiers not here?
        Dragonfly is designed to autonomously fly and land,
        has hazard detection to keep safe. Part of cosmic plan?

Are funds for environment needed more here?
We face extinction if we do not change.
Who are we to go to Titan and interfere?
Would Titan beings not welcome the exchange?
        Perhaps it is not the best idea.
        Concentrate on sustaining Gaia?

Naming Exoplanets

The naming of celestial objects is usually an exclusive affair. For its 100th anniversary the International Astronomical Union is letting the world vote. Dennis Overbye

There are more stars in the observable universe
than grains of sand on Earth- trillions upon trillions
enough for every human who ever lived to name a galaxy.

They need more names than for every imagined
creature. Astronomers usually give exoplanets numbers
with a letter or two like most celestial objects.

The I.A.U. released a list of stars and their planets
for 79 countries that signed up. The US has a yellow
star named HD17156 in constellation Cassiopeia.

It is certainly an unlivable furnace, three times
the mass of Jupiter. It orbits the host star
every 21 days and can be seen by small telescope.

Every country of the world can name its own planet
and the star it calls home. The process of naming
has begun. A contender Wilwarin from Tolkien.

Wilwarin is elvish name for Cassiopeia and Sauron.
Think of all the languages and possibilities. 4000
possible exoplanets in the Milky Way alone.

Spacecraft like NASA's Kepler and Tess and telescopes
on the ground speculate there could be billions of habitable
worlds in our galaxy alone. The I.A.U. stresses cooperation

and no political string-pulling or money paid
to a commercial star registry. Earthlings will vote
for names for 14 stars and 31 planets orbiting them.

We now have a four-planet system named for Cervantes–
Quixote, Dulcinea, Rocinante and Sancho in Ara constellation.
In Ursa Major: Taphao Thong and Tapho Kaew from Thai legend.

Each country is responsible for forming a committee
and organizing their own campaigns. Cultural and historical
indigenous names are encouraged.

The NameExoplanetWorld initiative reminds us
we are all together under one sky. We can choose
their official names. I am exited to see what names we choose.

Waves of the Future

Life comes at us in waves.
We can't predict or control those waves,
but we can learn to surf.

Dan Millman

Global Empowerment

As much as I believe with all my heart about the killing, the taking of innocent lives, I also believe that I will never support giving white legislators who have no interest in our community the ability to tell our women what they can do with their bodies. Rev. Clinton Stancil

As much as I believe you have the right to your opinion,
your comments as a male still are not as important
as women's own power and views about their bodies.

Male-hierarchical religions who dictate women's fates
and political leaders who do not support gender freedom
oppress women in many matters and endeavors.

So many wars, cultural norms are fought to appease men.
Disenfranchised women have not been able to reach
equity in most areas. The loss to progress is incalculable.

#MeToo and so many climate change initiatives
require incorporating everyone in facing
the challenges to our planet and survival.

Male outworn, privileged behaviors, insensitivity,
greed, misplaced intentions have caused
misery, injustice and sustainability problems globally.

This is much more than one's feelings about abortion.
Who gives anyone the power to disempower choice?
Incompetent leaders destroy our freedom to express.

We are all in this together and we need all voices
and talents. Women are made to feel not enough.
There is not enough respect for women.

How many eons does it take for humanity to wake up?
How many unfulfilled lives lost to prejudice?
We do not have time to waste on stupidity.

I hope we can become "woke" before it is too late.
Women–unite, claim your due. Men-shape-up,
cooperate. Create a future worth living for.

International Student Strike Day

We've stolen our children's future-and we're still stealing it. Jane Goodall

Today the students are striking, leaving classes,
marching for their future with community supporters
holding signs, marching and chanting with them.

Youth can see the damage done by waste,
greed, lack of responsibility for sustainability.
They want to breathe, restore viability.

Youth can see species disappearing, forests
in flames, plastic pollution, industrial smoke
and particulates, fossil fools, inaction.

Youth can see we do not recycle, conserve,
balance resources. Politicians are bought
to continue special lethal practices.

Youth can see the Environmental Protection
Agency rescinding Clean Air and Water acts,
increasing emissions, leaders entering wasteful wars.

Youth want to act and not passively accept
what their elders impose upon them. Why
die in oil wars? Why expect extinction?

Youth want a change in policies. They
want regenerative agriculture, closed loop
manufacturing and extraction processes.

Youth want renewable energy, carbon tax,
reduced use of fossil fuels. Invest in education
and health rather than death and destruction.

Youth see billions of people threatened
and somehow having to come together to save
themselves and all life on the planet.

Youth everywhere are striking, dangling
from bridges, challenging corporations,
raising their voices, risking for a future.

Youth are standing up for what they love
and want to live with. Time for everyone
to stand, strike and march with them.

If the world was cool, we'd be in school.

Marching for a Future

Oh when the youth
coming marching in
oh when the youth
come marching in.
I want to be in that number
when the youth come marching in.

Oh when the youth
strike for climate action
Oh when the youth
march out of class
I want to join in that number
when the youth strike, alas.

Oh when the youth
take a stand and shout,
Oh when the youth
chant their fears.
I want to hold a sign with them
and wipe away their tears.

Oh when the youth
yell "We vote next"
Oh when they expect adults to act
to see they have a future,
I want to vote with them, react—
when the youth yell "We vote next".

Oh when the youth
around the world strike
Oh when the youth expect
leaders to be responsible.
I want to take responsibility
when the youth expect me to.

Challenging Complacent Moral Cowards

Political will is a renewable resource and must be summoned in this fight. The American people are sovereign, and I am hopeful that they are preparing to issue a command on the climate to those who purport to represent them, " Lead, follow, or get out of the way". Al Gore

Should-have-been President Al Gore
could have lead us in a sustainable direction.
He believes we have the tools to do more
to slow global warming, change political selection.
> Listen to the science, youth cry.
> They want a future, not to die.

Could have lead us in a sustainable direction
if the election was won by popular vote.
We could have had earlier climate correction,
listened to the cause he wants to promote.
> We have leadership which regresses,
> undoes many of climate successes.

He believes we have the tools to do more,
to change patterns of food production,
manufacturing waste, carbon threats we ignore,
fewer births for population reduction.
> High temperatures fire migrations,
> floods, drought, destabilize many nations.

To slow global warming, change political selection
to progressive, proactive leaders, to moderate extremes.
All lives on Earth are seeking protection.
Some hope it is not as dire as it seems.
> Daily 140 million tons of pollution into sky.
> Weather is changing. Have we the will to try?

Listen to the science, youth cry
as they march and strike for a better deal.
Global values have gone awry.
Extinction now appears quite real.
> Fossil fuels need to stay in the ground.
> Other power sources have been found.

They want a future, not to die.
A regenerative agricultural revolution,
moves toward more sustainability, deny
a crisis will not lead to a solution.
> Can we remove greed, payoffs, corporate crime?
> Reconfigurations are slow. Can we act in time?

Pausing and Learning

*The world keeps getting hotter and faster and madder, and we don't pause, we
don't think, we don't learn, we just keep racing on to the next disaster.*
Edith on "Years and Years."

Do we have the time to pause and learn
until the final freeze or burn?

Do too many of us disagree
how to protect humanity?

Can we reconnect and refocus?
Realize it is not all about us?

Does the past provide ways we can nurture,
guidance to provide for descendants' future?

Will the cosmos send a blast
to end it all–really fast?

Is this world of dualistic, 3D
only part of multiversal reality?

Are we just a speck, a universal ort
in an experiment with an incomplete report?

Have we taken enough time to learn and pause?
Failed the test? Planet with predetermined clause?

I Wish I Could Write an Anthem

I wish I could write an anthem
for the youth of the world protesting
and marching for their future.

As they become more aware of the dire
threats–the climate emergency, waste,
gun violence, injustice, plastic, fossil fuels...

The list goes on and they can't vote,
they can't control adult conduct.
All they can do is speak up and stand up.

Will they take over the reins in time
to make the changes we need for
a safer, more equitable, sustainable world?

My time is nearly up and I have little power.
I march in a wheelchair, support just causes,
advocate for equal rights. It's not enough.

All people of good intention need an anthem
a rallying cry to empower change– a bonding
anthem to strengthen the will to survive.

I see the starving, caged children, traumatized
by war, shootings, lack of protection,
children dying before they can dream or act.

Too many of us using too many of Gaia's
resources, depleting flora and fauna,
poisoning the air, land and water.

How can I confront so many problems
to express such pain yet retain hope?
I wish I could write an anthem.....
            to make a difference.

Shifting Shadows

This sunny / overcast afternoon
shifts the backyard in and out of shadows.
Wind-chased clouds free the sun.

A few yellow clover and dandelions
prostrated before the mover and survived.
The windfall apples must have fallen afterward.

Apples are so abundant they require daily
pick-up. We need to find more friends
with horses. We can't store them all.

Since they are organic they are scaly,
bruised and wormy. My husband just
gouges out any imperfections.

Birds peck barkdust in the shade.
The lacy limb patterns on the grass
darken and lighten–disappear, surprise.

The temperature changes when shaded.
I change my chair so my back bakes in sun.
I need to protect my shadowed face from exposure.

Politically, we battle dark against light.
Moods shift with circumstances.
Sometimes it is hard to see light in darkness.

Humanity is shadowed by threats of extinction
with dark forces denying we have a problem.
As I muse, I can't see beyond the backyard fence.

But my mind and heart range globally,
probe cosmically, yearning for light.
Shadows shift until all is dark.

Earth's Lungs Smoking

Our concern is that if the forest is gone, people will also end.
Waipi Chief Ajareaty or Nazare.

The Amazon rainforest is a carbon sink
and produces 20% of Earth's oxygen.
Brazil is setting the forests on fire.

The loggers, farmers and miners
also slaughter the wildlife, threaten
indigenous peoples. The planet smokes.

A Waipi woman chief, Nazare is trying
to protect the rainforest, she travels
around the world to appeal for help.

13% of Brazil is protected indigenous land,
mostly in the Amazon, reserved for 900,000
indigenous people, once numbering millions.

Nations want to protect their future
and offer to help. But a Trumpian
president promotes greed, entitlement.

He wants to integrate indigenous people
into his society and open up their rich,
preserved lands for development. Meanwhile

the forest burns, wastes away, smoke
rises and clogs the atmosphere. Who
can make the chain smokers quit?

Planetary citizens are outraged, but
they can not shame or appeal to
the integrity of this president who has none.

Gaia puffs away, breathing becomes labored—
no respite on land, air, or sea. Non-smokers
inhale second-hand smoke nonetheless.

If only our tears could put out the flames.
If only countries would face climate crisis in time.
But, it only remains a pipe dream which puffs smoke.

145

Earth's "Second Lung" Inflamed

Earth's "First Lung" in the Amazon
is burning because of development,
but Brazil will not accept global leaders' help.

Earth's "Second Lung" is in Africa.
It too is burning. They are less equipped
technologically and financially to put fires out.

Most at risk is the Congo Basin forest,
which absorbs tons of carbon dioxide which
is key to the fight against climate change.

Brazil's fires race through environmentally
critical rainforest. In Africa the fires are at fringes
of rainforest, in savannah and scrubbier land.

Both lungs help us all breathe. Global Forest
Watch data and satellite map shows Africa as
a thick fiery splotch, the Amazon a dense red mass.

Rising temperatures, decreased rain, logging,
farming and mining increase the blazes.
The whole world needs to help the lungs breathe.

As climate change creeps into more dry areas,
we get ghastly fires, giant hybrid tumbleweeds
which attack inhabited lands, scare people there.

We get remnants of smoke in our valley at times.
North from Canada, south from California–smoke
funnels into our green, lush valley and chokes us.

Nowhere to escape the changes in nature
and human behavior. Denial is doom.
Cooperative solutions could help us breathe.

Waves of Smoke

It's really incredible how much the U.S. has managed to clean up the air from other pollution sources like power plants, and industry and cars. Climate change is throwing a new variable against our other efforts to clear the air through regulations. This is a kind of unexpected source of pollution and health hazard. Loretta Mickley

Severe waves of smoke from wildfires
sometimes lasting weeks longer than past,
spread on cross-country winds.

The ill effects from Southern California
through Canada and Alaska cause heart
attacks, breathing problems and other maladies.

Microscopic particles penetrate deeply into
the lungs causing coughing, chest pain and asthma
attacks. Children and elderly are most at risk.

Residents of Northern California, western Oregon,
and the Northern Rockies suffer the worst increases
in smoke exposure. Air purifiers and masks needed.

Ashland, Oregon has 40 days of smoke canceling
outdoor Shakespeare plays. Our choices are to stay
inside or flee. Seek smoke-free shelters–where?

Populations in unhealthy areas get alerts.
But Paradise, California suffered 146 deaths,
lost 35,000 houses and other structures.

Thick smoke drifts into cities. Massive
clouds bring health threats and breathing
problems, endangering and killing people.

Coal-fired power plants closures and fewer old cars
are helping, but wildfires increase. Satellite imagery
tries to predict where smoke travels and how intense.

With climate changes, more areas become prone
to wildfires. Smoke invades our Willamette Valley.
We have an air filter, masks, stay indoors.

Yet, Republican Oregon senators boycott a vote
to protect our state's environment and Trump destroys
progress made to contain coal and wilderness mining.

Around the world we suffer from unbreathable air.

Flugscham

Flugscham is German for shame of flying and the pollution it brings about.

Environmental activist Greta Thunberg is crossing
the Atlantic in a solar-powered, non-polluting sailboat.
She does not fly and on land uses trains.

Flugsham could apply to all polluters, excess
use of fossil fuels for destination weddings
and drivers of gas guzzling vehicles...shame.

Can shaming influence deniers and people
who feel privileged? The climate crisis
faces inaction and hypocrisy. A shame.

Flying has become so unpleasant for passengers
they might seek alternatives without shaming.
My last flight will be my last by choice...unashamed.

How effective is shaming in modern times?
What behavior brings shame? Abusers of all
kinds need to stop by many means. Shameful.

Climate change is a climate crisis. Global
warming is global heating. Time to step up
the language to alert people to act. Can we shame?

All priorities are pointless if we are extinct.
Our leaders are leading us to the brink.
Everyone must do their parts. Such a shame.

When we cannot breathe, drink or eat it will
be too late to fly anywhere. If we fly by
the seat of our pants–ass burns. Flugscham.

World Population Day

The planet's peccable people
have reached over 7.7 billion
and rising, impacting Gaia's livability.

On the fifth of an acre we steward,
I ponder the prospects in my overcast
backyard with intermittent shadows.

The spruce tosses cones to lump
the lawn. Tiny apples fall before
full growth, bump the grass.

We do not water our lawn in summer
to conserve water. The brown spots
revive in fall rains. Less mowing.

Two dandelions landed safely
on top of the rock wall and above
the thirsty lowlanders- yellow clover.

The sunflowers climb in overdrive.
No pesticides for visiting creatures.
Deer gated out to protect fruit.

Are we trying enough to advocate
for a sustainable planet? We have
too many people needing resources.

The billions of beings create waste
and destruction. Friction explodes
with climate change pressures.

Our population is out of control.
Will disease, nuclear war, natural
catastrophes curb our excesses?

How long will I be able to deep breathe,
contemplate in this tiny patch? We are all
part of Gaia's ecosystem. All connected.

I return inside to filtered, temperature
controlled air. We are now all electric.
Someday air— unbreathable. Power off.

When the Bough Breaks...
...When the bough breaks the cradle will fall. Nursery Rhyme

Overbearing apples broke their bough.
Weight of the overly-endowed
ripening fruit reached the breaking point.

The limb littered the lawn. Downed apples joined
windfalls. Unwatered grass is a prickly bed.
My husband stoops to tenderly pick apples up.

Into a white bucket he puts the downfalls
and carries them to the compost pile.
Too early to eat, they will decay.

Soon we'll call in friends to gather apples
for cider and to feed horses. We can't handle
all the apples burgeoning in the canopy.

The Homo sapiens branch of the family tree
(relatives were lopped off) after cradled in civilization,
could join the compost heap of Homo history.

We are billions taxing Gaia's resources.
Plastic piles. Polluted air, water, land
exploited unsustainably to final comedown.

Our organic yard is a start. We pruned for
this apple abundance. The sunflowers stretched
to the top of the weathervane, produces first bloom.

But if humanity is too fruitful and exploits Gaia
beyond capacity, our downfall is imminent.
Who will reseed the planet?

My husband rescued the one ripe peach from nearly
barren, struggling tree. The peach tree was watered,
warmly nurtured as we all hope to be.

Headlines

I scan the newspaper headlines,
decline to dig deeper into negative
articles and to wallow in despair.

I do not want to repeat the leads
into greed, deceit, degradation,
which squash the human spirit.

I move to the arts section, notable
New York Times obituaries which
highlight some illuminaries.

We need enlightening reading
about creative, uplifting endeavors
to help us cope and hope.

I screen what I see on television
and computers as well. I cannot
carry such darkness and weight.

Can't we focus on construction
not destruction? Act on solutions
and not on devolution?

Youth are restless for a future which
their elders have stolen from them
by their un-sustainable goals.

How much bad news can we absorb?
The headlines cross-out progress,
their words zipper us mute and helpless.

Taking Responsibility

Gurus urge taking responsibility for myself,
community and Earth with a sense of urgency.
I need to get moving and leap off the shelf.
The planet faces a global emergency.
       I'm overwhelmed with what's expected.
       My lack of energy I've detected.

Community and Earth with a sense of urgency
needs to connect to make a future viable.
Many people see an awakened insurgency
for the Old World Order has been unreliable.
       Do we get cleansing with a clean sweep?
       What to toss and what to keep?

I need to get moving and leap off the shelf
not easy when arthritic and domestically dusty.
I'm more Mother Time than spritely elf.
My mood crusty and my joints rusty.
       But I know I must help to nurture
       if my grandchildren are to have a future.

The planet faces a global emergency
in sustainability, climate change and leadership.
Can we mount a responsible resurgency?
Put down the screens and encourage readership?
       Can we become informed, avoid denial?
       It's as if we are all being put on trial.

I'm overwhelmed with what's expected.
How much can I donate, petition, or march?
Is the situation even worse than suspected?
Will we flood, burn, plastic-ize or parch?
       The time line for us to act is short.
       Time for us to show up and report.

My lack of energy, I've detected
makes me engage at lower and slower pace.
Can I fulfill duties I've selected?
How many more challenges do I face?
       They keep saying we are "enough"
       I wonder if we have the right star stuff.

How Dare You?

How dare you. You have stolen my dreams and my childhood with your empty words...We will not let you get away with this. Right now is where we draw the line.
Greta Thunberg at United Nations Climate Action Summit. September 23, 2019

The eyes of all future generations are upon you.
Even if all nations followed through with commitments...
Even with limiting future warming to another
0.72 degrees Fahrenheit from now it is not enough.
Even if we have 50% chance those odds are not good enough.

If you choose to fail us, I say we will never forgive you.
No climate speech by Trump and he withdrew from Paris Climate
Agreement, has repealed U.S. carbon-reduction policies.
With three-minute speeches other leaders made promises
for climate policies, but so far most countries fall short.

Our young people understand climate change is no
longer up for debate–it's a reality based in science.
Four million around the world marched for a future.
D.C. protesters clogged traffic. Still some deniers,
delays, inaction by leaders. Fox news called her mentally
ill and said liberal adults were indoctrinating youth
for their agenda. They do not assume responsibility.

"I should be in school on the other side of the ocean.
Yet you have come to us young people for hope."
Will the world listen in time? Economic growth
fossil fuels, waste could shave 10 % of U.S.
economy by century's end, federal report states.
She has learned the seas are rising, the weather
worsens, more fires and floods, more migrations.

Greta told it straight, enraged at the inaction
when we have known for over thirty years
we were headed for extinction if we did not
change our ways. Fossil fuels fight renewables.
As the world dawdles the clock ticks.
How much future does Greta or any of us have?

Greta said, "Everyone said, We hear you but they
are tone deaf." Meanwhile youth strike Fridays,
marches of the community go global. We all
should be shaking our head and shouting,
"How dare you?" Where's moral courage?

Imaginary Worlds

Imagination will often carry us to worlds that never were, but without it we go nowhere. Carl Sagan

Our imaginations create new worlds in fantasy and fiction.
Utopias we can dream will come true. Inventions can aid.
Our ancient ancestors would find today puzzling.

We can simulate realities on screens,
see a virtual reality with many options.
TV, movies, plays let us escape the mundane.

Perhaps we can imagine a sustainable,
achievable future, solving problems
of poverty, injustice, inequality?

With billions of people pressuring the planet,
draining resources, polluting and wasting, this world
seems endangered. How can we act together?

Some gurus say we will transition to the Fifth Dimension.
No time lines and maybe not all will go. What is this
Golden Age like? An imaginative leap? Possibility?

We can't just jet into space to exploit elsewhere.
Even if we transfer consciousness to robots.
The fleshy parts of us add to the rot here.

Have our cosmic cousins advanced civilization
to the point they might help us out? They would
have to be true humanitarians.

I can imagine many worlds, experience dream
realities. I believe I'm multidimensional. I may
be living simultaneous lives in many dimensions.

If my soul is eternal, have I ever lived in a tranquil,
free-thinking, cooperative place? Will I ever?
In my mind I can, but I'll leave body-baggage behind.

Waves of Celebration

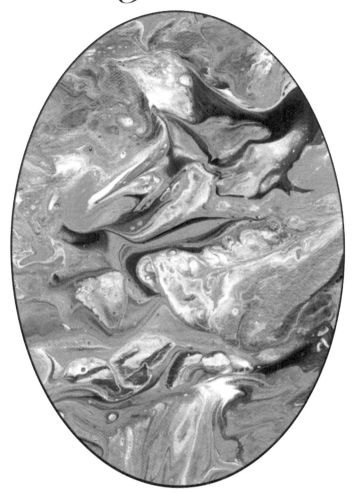

Being creative on the waves
is challenging
but we each create art
in our own way.

Bethany Hamilton

Observing Earth Day

As I file my Earth Day backyard report,
I must apologize for my car farts
polluting your air en route to exercise class.

The sun sparkles the dew on the grass–
a partial substitute for the mowed dandelions
which a humming bumblebee searches for in vain.

Bummed out bee has no floral GPS, as randomly
he squiggles across the lawn, frenetically
scouting gold spots–finding not even a puffball.

Apple and pear blossoms expand daily.
Plum and peach buds have not even leafed.
The latter, covered by crusty crud, show iffy potential.

Red azalea and white strawberry blooms
plus blue pinwheel hint patriotism, but green,
purple and browns reveal I am a Gaia patriot.

The wind chimes and pinwheel follow wind
rhythms. The pinwheel's shadow flickers
as it shifts positions, sifts sun.

A tuft of pale lichen–a lonely ship on green sea.
Birds of all sizes and voices flit and perch.
I spot a dug-up dandelion on top of the compost pile.

I like to call you, our planet Gaia–sounds more motherly
than Mother Earth. Earth sounds harsh more fatherly.
All creatures and manifestations are your children.

As I sit leisurely on my chi chair surveying
our small domain gifted with life, I anguish
about people who are such destructive stewards.

As people march around the world for action
on climate change and the end of fossil fuels,
mining, plastics–dare I hope we act in time?

No one should deny we have disrespected,
destroyed, abused our Mother Gaia. I can only
advocate for better treatment for our nurturer.

Love and light from your devoted supporter and fan.

Dreaming Reality

A dream you dream alone is only a dream. A dream you dream together is reality.
John Lennon

With Woodstock we learned when a dream
is shared, a reality can be experienced
of our hopes for peace and love... briefly.

People say it can only happen once
with 400,000 strangers helping each
other under trying conditions.

Woodstock 50 could not be realized
due to landowners not willing to give them
space to try again–even if more organized.

Like inventions and creative endeavors
the dream of one gets shared and enters
a wider reality. Billions of possible receivers.

Many young people can't dream of a future
due to environmental threats caused
by humanity's abuse and misuse.

How do we get billions of people
to dream of a peaceful, sustainable world?
The challenges appear overwhelming.

People may not have the same dreams.
Can we balance conflicting realities?
Any consensus or more conflicts?

Gurus suggest we start with ourselves
to be the change we want to see. But
we need others to join together to progress.

So many different intentions in our nation,
let alone all the other countries. Why
was humanity seeded here anyway?

Persisting and resisting is exhausting,
especially for the elderly. What dreams
will our descendants have, if they survive?

We can support the light-bringing organizations
trying to create a better world. As long as we
can dream, there is hope?

Go Greta!
Be like Greta.
On a sweatshirt of a well-wisher. Unite Behind the Science: Greta Thunberg

Sixteen year old Swedish climate change activist
Greta Thunberg sets sail today in a solar-powered,
emission-free sailboat from Plymouth, England to New York.

The expected two-week trek across the Atlantic
will take her to the United Nations Climate Talks
then on to Chile and other climate events.

The Maliza II carries a small crew, Greta and
her father. She has freeze-dried vegetarian fare.
She packed many books, has eight writing journals.

Disconnected from Internet, there is a satellite phone
to send her pictures. The instigator of student
walkouts for climate change is taking a year off school.

She will drink desalinated water, use a bucket
toilet. She and her father will have beds, but
the crew will sleep on beanbags.

She is anxious about the trip and will miss her dogs,
but the emissions from flying are too damaging and
polluting. As tipping points come, she fights for a future.

She is autistic, Asperger syndrome and suffered from
depression so severe she could not eat and stopped growing.
Yet, she is focused on making humanity responsible.

To the young men who choose violence and
white supremacy to deal with their depression,
perhaps you could emulate Greta and non-violence?

We do not have a future if we all do not work together.
The replacement we all face is extinction and perhaps
a re-seeding with species who will steward Gaia?

Greta has been nominated for the Nobel Peace Prize.
I hope she wins like Malala. These young women could
help us survive– not the demented, anti-women young men.

New Moon Eclipse in July

On July 2nd, just before the 4th, some predict
a profound doorway opening to receive downloads
of expanded consciousness and higher awareness.

You can reset into your next level of soul truth
and destiny, but this energy may feel challenging
if you are feeling challenged, emotional, a bit off.

Supposedly we have access to an infinite well
of peace and Divine presence within. Quiet your mind.
Open your heart. And tune in. Good luck.

Meanwhile, I'm wary of fireworks blasts starting forest
fires, injuring enthusiasts in unsafe conditions. I wish
they'd ban fireworks except by pros in safe areas.

Why not artistic drone light shows like at the Olympics?
No smoke. No polluting air. Environmentally better
for us all. Patriotism does not demand explosives.

So if I manage to obtain some of these beneficial
eclipse enlightening waves, I still face challenging
light displays which don't improve the lives of anyone.

South America gets a glimpse of the eclipse this time.
We should get some remnant energy, if we can access
its positive potential. Let's hope it helps some of us.

Happy Cousin's Day: July 24th

Today is Happy Cousins Day.
Never heard of it until saw it on Bing
this morning before attacking emails.

So I was able to email two cousins
I keep in touch with, but I wonder about
other cousins. I don't know where they are.

Cousins come from parents' siblings
children. All my parents' brothers
and sisters are dead as are they.

When all were living-most on the east coast
they kept in touch and happily celebrated
holidays with Swedish traditions.

When I was young I saw my cousins
at family gatherings and celebrations,
famous for long hugs-Anderson's goodbyes.

They assimilated non-Swedish spouses
at the potluck weekend gatherings. Many came
to New Britain by streetcars long ago.

My mother and her three sisters were
especially close and tried to maintain
contact even as they moved away.

My cousins and I were busy growing up,
away at school, marrying and moving.
I only see one cousin in person, occasionally.

My children and grandchildren have few cousins
they see often. Cousins are a warm link to our
family tree. We shared grandparents.

I have so many memories of times when
the extended family could be together.
On a trip to Connecticut this spring,

I missed all the departed family members
and the abundant smorgasbords. I cherish
cousins and all the relatives remaining.

World Emoji Day

Apple and Google are rolling out dozens of new emoju that include cute critters, of course, but also expand the number of images of human diversity.
Michelle Chapman

Apple's holding hands emoji can have 75
variations in gender and skin color: prosthetic
arms and legs as well as wheelchairs,
a new guide dog and ear with hearing aid.

There is a yawning emoji (probably
from looking at all the images). New animals
are sloth, flamingo, skunk, orangutan.
All to celebrate World Emoji Day.

Google has 71 couple versions with different
skin tones. They have a diva lamp
so for Diwali can be celebrated
along with Christmas and Thanksgiving.

Anyone can create an emoji, but to make it
to phones and computers it must be approved
by Unicode–people from large companies. It will
look the same no matter where it is sent globally.

Emoji images can be interpreted, read, but not
spoken. It is an international language. A drop
of blood, probing cane, kneeling person, oyster,
eggplant, parachute can have several nuances.

The digital generation, especially loves sending emoji
to express a wide range of emotion. My hands
work with words and produce images, not draw
images to evoke words. Whatever connects.

My elderly friends might send a smiley face at
the end of an e-mail or a heart. I am high-tech
enough to understand it, but not adept at finding
emoji to send back or write sentences with them.

Fourth of July Observations

This noon-ish, sunny Fourth of July,
I carry Bottom, a newly refurbished,
concrete angel back to his backyard pad.

He's spruced up his act–newly cleansed
of his hazelnut seed-pod necklace, the dirt
and grime of seasonal detritus.

The blue tabletop beside my chair has been
scrubbed for Bottom, who is now clear-coated
and shiny– protected from the elements.

I sit and smile at his transformation. I hope
chi flows energy through me, activates my chakras,
lets me lighten up and shine.

The grass seems to be having a bad hair day.
Strands poke in all directions at different heights,
some bent and some standing tall.

One un-pulled, un-mowed dandelion about a foot
tall is a beacon of perseverance. Two puffballs
near the rock wall proceeded to re-seed.

The untended, white weed bucket awaits
the groundskeeper beside tiny mushrooms
in a precarious spot. I'm rooting for them.

My husband postpones weeding to nibble
his delicious abundant blueberries. He isn't
into sharing with birds or other creatures.

The birds chatter in the branches and poke ground.
Like newly watered blueberries and azaleas we hope
the hydrated peach tree makes more of an effort.

I move my chair onto the lawn, my back to the sun,
hoodie up to protect my face. The sun warms
my back to my core. I become a curiosity for bugs.

I pick up a shiny blue and gray feather.
I admire its beauty and potential good omen.
The upward pattern is uplifting.

A neighbor shoots off a few small fireworks.
A big bang blasts in the distance. A plane
gives us a preview of upcoming flybys.

I am not in favor of the military flare of Trump's
parade–tanks tearing up the streets, flyovers
boasting of military might. I won't watch.

Instead I will watch Macy's display on TV,
and hope non-polluting celebrations someday
reflect an awareness of climate changing times

Our red roses beside blue and white pinwheel
reside peacefully side by side. A gentle breeze
tickles the wind-chimes' quiet anthem.

I pat Bottom on his head as I take my feather
inside to put with other found feathers in my new
wooden cup–a work of art made from Oregon Alder.

Festive for the Fourth of July

Across the nation people gather to watch parades,
fireworks, attend barbecues, fireworks displays, visit
friends and family. It is a holiday for freedom.

In D.C. it rained on Trump's parade. He spouted
static tanks on streets
and flyovers to display military might.

But in town's and cities there were less bombastic
celebrations, more community-based gatherings
for people who hope democracy improves and prevails.

Corvallis has a quirky tradition called the Everyone-Can-Join,
Fabulous, Fantastic Fourth of July Parade. 3,000 spectators
watched over 800 participants for the 34th year.

Pedal-powered vehicles, bikes, trikes, Kid's Kinetic
Challenge–a combo of art on people-powered wheels.
A fire truck, police car, decorated cars and trucks.

People costumed in red-white and blue, Lady Liberty,
all-ages walking behind an off-center banner. They sang
The Star-Spangled Banner and then they were off.

Various organizations touted health care for all,
Republicans were a no-show, but Democrats had
a pick-up truck with Bernie Sanders posters,

a life-sized cut-out with the slogan: "The more
you learn, the more you Bern." Local politicians
also strut their stuff in the parade.

The first group was a gaggle of patriotic kids
followed by adults–some pushing strollers, pulling wagons.
All ages waving, to watchers. One child was a fairy,
another a tennis ball, a unicorn. One adult a mermaid.

Bagpipes played Scottish music. Dog-lovers
with their pets, paraders tossing candy, families
dressing up in theme costumes, decking up vehicles.

From past years I liked the kazoos, various bands.
Each year is its own blend of creative conglomerations.
Next year I'd like to see marchers promote climate change.

Women's World Cup Soccer Team Shines
   at Ticker-Tape Parade in New York City

Red, white and blue paper flakes flurried
around the women in their world champion
shirts and blue-ribboned metals.

All ages and genders lined the streets,
traveling long distances to cheer
the triumphant women, spraying champagne.

Jubilant poses, radiant smiles exchanged
with the magnificent athletes and strong advocates
for the empowerment of women and equal pay.

People shouted "equal pay" in the arena
and at FIFA officials. Megan Rapinoe
gave a stirring speech. Some of the points–

> "Got pink hair and purple hair.
> We have tattoos and dreadlocks.
>   We got white girls and black girls
> and everything in between.
> Straight girls and gay girls..."

> "It is my absolute honor to lead this team
> on the field. There is no place I would
> rather be–even in the presidential race.
> I'm busy. I'm sorry." (She out-polled Trump)

> "This is my charge to everyone.
> We have to do better. We have
> to love more and hate less.
> We got to listen more and talk less.
> It is our responsibility to make the world
> a better place. We have to collaborate.
> It takes everybody."

> "This is my charge to everybody.
> Do what you can. Do what you have to do.
> Step outside yourself. Be more, be better,
> be bigger than you've ever been before."

I could not be prouder of these shining examples
of what you can achieve when you do your best.
Little girls are dyeing their hair purple and pink,
ready to stand up to play on a level playing field.

Why Angels?

I have to believe in angels because
their presence provides me some comfort.
They seem part of my life chart, cosmic clause.
Perhaps they guide and support my effort.
  Whether they are true or not,
   imagining them lifts my earthly slot.

Their presence provides me some comfort
that perhaps there is light somewhere in multiverse.
Are they my enlightened cosmic consort?
Keep me being better than worse?
  Wings and feathers may be an illusion.
   Just a concept not a real conclusion.

They seem part of my life chart, cosmic clause,
a way to enhance our All connection.
They seem to receive global applause—
a part of diverse cultural, spiritual selection.
  We yearn to uplift, take flight.
  We yearn to escape earthly blight.

Perhaps they guide and support my effort
to perform my perceived mission for why I'm here.
I am just conscious energy in an eternal ort,
looking for a clear atmosphere.
  Angels do not have to exist for me
  to seek their light-bringing possibility.

Whether they are true or not
I persist in believing in their radiant shine.
No proofs could ever blot
out my commitment. Angels are mine.
  I can conjure them whenever I need to.
  They are the consolers I plead do.

Imagining them lifts my earthly slot.
I can see light beings sparkling the dark.
They remind me of beings I forgot?
Angels prevent darkling my mark?
  When I think of angels, I smile
  and feel perhaps this lifetime's worthwhile.

166

Waves of 53

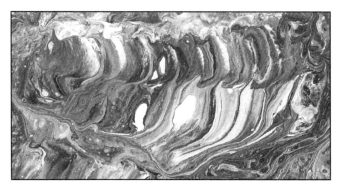

Meaning of 53

53 is a combination of courage and creativity.
53 is a 2-digit number composed
of the vibrations of 5 and 3,
a positive and powerful number
characterized by great creativity.

Freedom, energy, progress
and motivation
means success.

Fast adaptation, courage
to life's decisions,
to engage.

With communicativeness
and resourcefulness
you'll impress.

53 sounds great
to create.

Linda Varsell Smith

Fifty-Three

With syllables fifty-three,
a new rhymed form of
poetry.

Three triplets that must rhyme first
and third lines, then couplet
if well-versed.

Fun to word-play with best words,
to fit the pattern
for word-nerds.

Poetry lights way,
every day

Meaning of 53

53 is a combination of courage and creativity. 53 is a 2-digit number
composed of the vibrations of 5 and 3, a positive and powerful number
characterized by great creativity.

Freedom, energy, progress
and motivation
mean success.

Fast adaptation, courage
to life decisions
to engage.

With communicativeness
and resourcefulness,
you'll impress.

53 sounds great
to create.

Can I Fly?

Once I thought I could fly low
over to my friend's house.
        Just let go.

I couldn't get rising lift
with my arms outspread.
        Could not drift.

I could visualize ride,
skimming above ground,
        joy inside.

Can I soar, explore
        anymore?

Taking Flight

Once I believed in fairies,
other sky beings.
        I'm Aries.

Now I believe in angels
with no reason why.
        Magicals?

It just makes me feel lighter.
Winged-ones lift spirits.
        Enlighter?

Will I lift higher?
        Inspire?

Life Stories

In the end, we'll all become stories. Margaret Atwood

We each live unique stories,
even record them.
Some glories?

Do we plot from a life chart?
We don't remember?
Free will start?

The challenges, surprises
tend to block our path,
we surmise?

Living in the light?
What's my plight?

The Big Questions

Who, what, why, when, how, we ask?
Why did we come here?
What is task?

Are we here to learn, to grow?
Make the world better?
Try to know?

Answers hard to find for me.
An eternal search?
Just earthly?

Do I connect to All
protocol?

Plea to my Guardian Angel

Bella, please relieve my pain,
clear fearful darkness,
light again.

Must pursue my life's mission.
I have little time.
Permission?

We all must pitch in to help
save Gaia's future.
Hear my yelp!

Have I your wrong name?
Face endgame?

Angels at Play

Do angels spin halo-loops?
Roll halos in clouds?
Halo-hoops?

Sing irreverent music?
Play loud instruments?
Dance with kick?

Visit forbidden places
to see the dark side?
Hide faces?

Wear a hip tattoo
just like you?

Advocates for Gaia

Youths want to have a future.
Endangered planet
needs nurture.

Globally they march for change.
Climate crisis looms–
world-wide range.

Some dense folks slow to react,
to sense urgency.
Wake up! Act!

More resolutions.
Solutions?

Be the Change
> *Never doubt that a small group of thoughtful, committed citizens can change the world, indeed, it's the only thing that ever has.* Margaret Mead

One by one become a batch.
Face the enemy
meet and match.

Form platform for alliance,
advocate for truth,
take a chance.

To make a positive change
speak up and be heard,
make exchange.

You are not alone
to dethrone.

Napping

When I'm tired, drained by pain,
I will take a nap to
rest my brain.

When writing I take a break,
ideas simmer,
while I ache.

I pour most my energy
when I'm creating
synergy.

Napping's a time out,
turnabout.

Sleepless in Corvallis

Do we need less sleep when old?
Body parts can leak?
Prone toward cold?

Dreams enlighten or turn dark?
Limbs go akimbo?
Disembark?

Go to other dimensions?
See our soul-slivers?
What intentions?

Why do I awake?
For whose sake?

Common Beliefs

I want you to feel the fear I feel every day. And then I want you to act. Greta Thunberg

People of faith or if not
have things in common,
tie the knot

for compassion and the Earth,
love of children
caring's worth?

If love children and the world
why the deniers?
Science hurled?

Act for a future
and nurture.

Lungs

Do not smoke, burn, pollute or vape.
Keep air breathable,
lungs in shape.

Forests are our world's carbon sink.
Earth's lungs are burning,
out of sync.

We huff and puff yucky stuff.
Clog up atmosphere.
We've enough?

Keep our lungs heaving.
We're leaving?

Totidem Verbis
   With just so many words. In these words.

With just so many words start
to build a new line,
fit a part.

In these words, chosen, succinct,
a new creation,
It's distinct.

Find a pattern or a form.
Place words within it
to perform.

When words afflated,
created.

Cooperative Scrabble

Poets gather to dabble
in nine-tile word-play
for Scrabble.

We all win, for don't keep score.
Board to tablecloth
to play more.

It's a bingo if use nine
tiles. Sonnetted is
best of mine.

We use all the tiles.
Word-nerd smiles.

Riding Waves of Light

As planet lifts to higher
energy, be less
deniers?

Galactic light codes are
beyond old patterns,
best so far?

Write with light codes, breathe, heal,
focus positive,
new reveal?

We'll begin anew?
Is it true?

Go with the Flow

Those supposedly who know
urge the new not old
just let go.

To connect with universe,
stay open to all,
and converse.

We are part of cosmic All.
Here on mission, learn
protocol.

Do we know our link?
You would think.

Holi: Spring Festival of Colors

Red: love and fertility.
Yellow: tumeric
Blue: godly

Krishna. Green: begin anew.
Liquid and powdered
colors threw.

They use water-based pigments
as they celebrate
good figments.

Triumph over evil.
No devil.

Feather Collector

I collect fallen feathers.
Perhaps good omens.
together?

Placed in wooden, carved jar.
They flare out like flames,
stellular.

Reminders of flight, to soar,
create openly,
to explore,

pluck luck, reduce stress–
happiness.

Soul Attentiveness

This is the first, the wildest, the wisest thing I know. The soul exists and is built entirely out of attentiveness. Mary Oliver

What is the soul's intention?
Witness? Does it seek
attention?

Can souls help sufferers heal?
Keep some things hidden
or reveal?

Is soul advised, fixed or saved?
Is the soul set free
or enslaved?

Does soul get chances
as enhances?

Ancient Wisdom

We restore world's wholeness now
one heart at a time?
We know how?

Develop and recognize
old hidden wisdom—
past is wise?

Connect to old world-wide web—.
Grandmother Spider's.
Never ebb.

Life is everywhere.
Be aware.

178

Predicting the Future

The best way to predict the future is to create it. Buckminster Fuller

If our billions create
futures, don't connect–
resonate

can you predict pure chaos?
Effect the planet?
The cosmos?

If only constant is change,
how can we predict?
Rearrange?

Create best you can
without plan?

Bioneers

To pioneer biologically, inventor of environmental solutions and biotechnology and crafter of creative solutions to environmental and socio-cultural problems.
Rachel Naomi Remen

The planet needs bioneers
to heal, restore—
pioneers.

Find hidden wholeness, bless life,
summon potential,
be midwife.

Are we made of the right stuff
to make difference?
We're enough?

Discover instinct
or extinct?

Self-Doubt

The worst enemy to creativity is self-doubt. Sylvia Plath

Was it her self doubt which lead
to her writing's end,
left her dead?

Did poetry keep her alive, free?
Creativity
was her plea?

What lead her to quench her flame?
Her blood jet fizzle?
Whose to blame?

Just what is self-doubt
all about?

Tools to Communicate

It's not enough to just give the people a voice, we need to make sure that people aren't using it to harm other people or spread misinformation...Across the board, we have a responsibility to not just build tools, but to make sure they are used for good.
Mark Zuckerberg.

With fake news, bad blogs and hacks,
we're deceived, derailed
off the tracks.

They're idiots on Twitter—
One orange, deranged,
dim critter.

No responsibility
to convey the facts,
decency.

Fact-check, trace the source.
No recourse.

Savor Dandelions

I love all dandelions,
radiating yard.
Sun's scions.

They are an herb not a weed.
Beautiful to me,
that bees need.

But my husband mows them down
instead of picks them.
Makes me frown.

Try salad, wine, tea!
Hear my plea!

Bletting

Ripening fruit is bletting
time for harvesting
begetting.

We only had one ripe peach,
few plums and more pears
out of reach.

Apples abundant, cherries
diseased and now gone—
just berries

Once had more bletting.
Forgetting?

Becoming Better

When we love, we always strive to become better than we are. When we strive to be better than we are, everything around us becomes better too. Paulo Coelho

What the world needs now is love?
And compassion?
A green glove?

Billions of people thrive,
sustain, protect, keep
hope alive?

We can do and be better.
Not easy to do.
Unfetter?

Could be love can grow.
Will we know?

Conformity

I think the reward for conformity is that everyone likes you except yourself.
Rita Mae Brown

If you don't compare or compete
people respect you?
You're complete?

You have right to make mistakes
and they are right too?
What's at stake?

If trying to be normal,
never grow outside box?
Informal?

So get off the shelf,
be yourself.

Getting In Sync

Everything is energetic. So we as humans are comprised of all these elements. And they all vibrate at different frequencies. And if something is out of sync, then you find something that will help the body, or that part of the body get back into perfect vibration. It could be crystals. It could be hands-on, taking my energy. It could be a plant that has a certain energy given to that person's body. It could be a detoxification program, getting rid of some of the things that are causing it. It could be certain herbs. It could be sunlight.
                    Dolores Cannon

I have tried them all some time.
I still carry pain.
Not my prime.

Wrong technique for the wrong part?
Not in sync with it?
Broken heart?

All sound very doable.
Can rejuvenate?
Enable?

I am out of sync.
Why you think?

Healing with Massage

She massages my blubber
with hands and warm stones.
I'm rubber.

I'm prone on a heated pad,
absorb energy
while unclad.

Wearing just my underpants,
skin soaks in the creams.
Chakras dance.

Light enters, dark goes.
My lymph flows.

Multiversal Genesis

Into the void of silence, into the empty space of nothing, the joy of life is unfurled. C.S. Lewis

Did All begin from nothing?
Glom into matter?
Did life spring?

Life a joy everywhere?
Raucous or quiet?
Or aware?

Is consciousness illusion?
A beginning or
conclusion?

I've no answers yet.
I forget?

Radio Image of Black Hole

55 million light years from Earth. 6.5 billion times more massive than our sun.

A super-massive black hole
seen in a shadow.
View it whole?

Gargantuan galaxy
M87
mystery.

Black holes emit no light so
telescope array
sees shadow.

Ravage out of sight?
Not our plight?

Becoming Desperate

I am becoming desperate for change now–not in 8 years or 12 years, but right now.
Michelle Obama

We're becoming desperate
about politics
or climate.

Don't we need a global change?
Are the solutions
out of range?

Leaders in charge are flawed.
Greedy deniers,
views outlawed.

Ruled by one percent.
No consent.

Berniestock

Monteith Riverpark Albany, Oregon
Bernie's Birthday September 8th 2019

Huge bubbles float across grass.
Children poke at them.
Burst alas.

Blaring band blasts music burn.
Bernie banners flare.
Rain tamps Bern.

Undercover booths' wares:
food, pamphlets, pins, shirts.
We're aware

country's in trouble.
Burst bubble.

Judging Poets

> *Poets are damned, but they are not blind. They see with the eyes of angels.*
> William Carlos Williams

Why are just the poets damned
and some have been blind,
their thoughts slammed?

Not sure how judgment will work?
By whom in what place?
Saint or jerk?

Angels align with all sorts?
Or are they choosy?
Just good sports?

Poets tend to enlight
and delight.

Kneeling

> *If you can only be tall because somebody is on their knees, then you have a*
> *serious problem.* Toni Morrison

Just for what are you bending?
Worship? Dominance?
What's trending?

Why aren't you standing tall?
Stalwart. Resolute.
Not so small?

Kneeling to garden, plant seed?
To Kill or nurture?
Remove weed?

Get off of your knees.
Who to please?

Sitting in the Backyard

In backyard, I gather chi
in shade, not in sun–
not daily.

I am a fair-weather friend,
when it's warm and dry–
won't pretend.

I huff deep breaths of fire,
observe seasons
I desire.

I'm fickle I'm told.
Don't like cold.

Vade Mecum
    Something a person carries about for frequent or regular use.

For many it's a cell phone.
Others consult a book.
Some screen prone.

Clothing a matter of taste
or need and perhaps
done in haste.

Deal with thoughts' destinations,
realizations or
sensations.

Pain, worries as well.
Hurts like hell.

Earth School

Earth is a school. It has different classrooms. Different classrooms carry different frequencies to support different expressions of culture knowing creativity. Each culture had its own music, its own language, and its own frequencies. Dolores Cannon

From indigenous wisdom
and ancient knowledge
to the bomb.

Now with billions in classes
just what will we learn?
Morasses?

What will we keep from the old?
What's brought with the new?
What's foretold?

Creativity
sets us free?

Earthly Facades

Apparently when we enter the Earth existence, the third dimensional reality, we exist with a facade as actors playing various roles. For some it is the adventure of the experience, the journey. For others it is entrapment in an illusion that takes on all the qualities of reality. Dolores Cannon

Free will helps decide factors
if we will be good,
bad actors?

Or are we trapped in a script
play unchosen role,
nondescript.

Adventure or illusion,
our choice is in the
conclusion?

I would like some say
who I play.

The Archaic Ones

For untold millennium they have traveled through the galaxies searching for planets that have reached the point where they could support life. Their job was to begin the life process. Then the developing species were left on their own because of the prime directive of non-interference. Dolores Cannon

Apparently intruders
came to spoil this test
uprooters?

Some DNA made dormant
now awakening.
Informant?

Creating a New Earth now?
Like Archaic Ones?
Cosmic show?

Are we avatars
to the stars?

Bubbles

Each being is like a shimmering bubble and all their knowledge together forms like electric currents that flow to the universes. To all the places that need it. And so a planet in trouble like Earth was, can call on that electricity to come to them. It comes like a golden current and it brings the healing. And it becomes available to the whole planet. Dolores Cannon

Let's blow some bubbles on Earth.
Burst them to heal us?
What's our worth?

Electric bubbles that flow,
many light bubbles.
Let us glow!

Universes share current?
Where the bubbles go,
apparent?

Shimmering bubble
en-bubble.

Awakening Our Essence

The awakening is the purpose. The awakening of the fact that in essence we are light, we are love. Each cell of our body, each cell and molecule of everything. The power source that runs all life is light. So to awaken to that knowledge, and to desire to operate in that realm, and to believe that it is possible, are all factors that will put you there.
Dolores Cannon

So many in sleepy dark
to awaken to light?
Disembark?

Can we imagine or know
a radiant realm?
Will we go?

Awakening to purpose
so wonderful, good?
Just suppose

it's permissible?
Possible?

Awakening

As we all awaken and raise our frequencies, we are helping each other and our Earth to accomplish her mission of raising frequencies to be fully in another dimension.
Dolores Cannon

Are we rising to 5D?
We're stuck in 3D?
In 4D?

If higher what will we gain?
Why must we change now?
New campaign?

Yes, Earth could use an uplift.
It is polluted.
Set adrift?

Asleep or awake,
lives at stake.

Bearable Through Love

For small beings such as we, the vastness is only bearable through love. Carl Sagan

To those below, from above
connections to All
forged in love?

If we are beings of light,
does love energy
beam us bright?

Such vastness beyond belief.
Just what is out there?
Love's relief?

Love is source of hope.
Helps us cope?

The Grand Experiment

We are the only planet that has been given free will. That is why we are called the "Grand Experiment". Then there is the prime directive of non-interference...The information and devices etc. are given to the people as a gift and then they stand back and watch and see how it will be used. It is the people's free will what they do with it and many times we didn't use it for the purpose intended. Dolores Cannon

So the Grand Experiment
governed by free will
evident?

But I'd hoped they'd intervene.
For we have flubbed up
as I've seen.

The cosmos made a mistake?
Put people in charge?
For whose sake?

Is this a theory?
Mystery?

Emergence

Thoughts don't come from "within"; neither do they come from "without".
They emerge "between". Bayo Atomolate

When inside meets outside, thought
forms between them both?
Least it ought?

Thought released by voice or hand?
Thought emerges so
understand?

In some way thought emerges
in bits and parts or
in surges?

So does it matter?
Thoughts scatter.

Traveling Light

While the body sleeps our soul or spirit is having many adventures. It may
travel to the spirit realm to meet with master teachers and guides to obtain
advice or to learn lessons. It also may travel to other parts of our world or even
venture outward to other worlds and dimensions. Dolores Cannon

When in my dream state travels,
awake thought process
unravels.

Out of body I lightly
explore other realms,
am spritely.

Dreams yes, nightmare no–please.
Want to know why, where,
be at ease,

remember places
other faces?

Painting and Poetry

Painting is a silent poem, and poetry is painting that speaks. Plutarch

When a painting speaks to you,
poetry revealed,
deja vu.

Images in poetry
paint visions and
clarify.

When together, they are art.
Inspire as whole
or apart.

They're a collection,
reflection.

Eternal Soul

Time being after all, only the current of the soul in its flow. D.H. Lawrence

What if all of time is now?
Is soul eternal?
I don't know.

Can I be all over place?
Another form? Just
human race?

Can I cosmically explore?
Become diverse, can
become more?

Act for my soul's sake?
Get a break?

Waves of Poetry

Other Poetry Books by Linda Varsell Smith

Cinqueries: A Cluster of Cinquos and Lanterns
Fibs and Other Truths
Black Stars on a White Sky
Poems That Count
Poems That Count Too
* Winging-It: New and Selected Poems
*Red Cape Capers: Playful Backyard Meditations
*Star Stuff: A Soul-Splinter Experiences the Cosmos
*Light-Headed: A Soul-Splinter Experiences Light
* Sparks: A Soul-Splinter Experiences Earth
* Into the Clouds: Seeking Silver Linings
*Mirabilia: Manifesting Marvels, Miracles and Mysteries
*Spiral Hands: Signs of Healing
*Lacunae: Mind the Gap
*Wayfinding: Navigating the Unknown
* Wordy-Smith: Dancing the Line
* Hugger-Muggery:Ways to Hugs and Mugs
* The Ground Crew: Beings with Earthly Experience

* Available at www.Lulu.com/spotlight/rainbowcom

Chapbooks

Being Cosmic, Intra-space Chronicles,
Light-Headed, Red Cape Capers

On-Line Web-site Books

Free-access @ www.RainbowComunications.org

Syllables of Velvet   Word-Playful   Poetluck

Anthologies

The Second Genesis, Branches, Poetic License,
Poetic License 2015, Jubilee, The Eloquent Umbrella

Twelve Novels in the Rainbow Chronicles Series